THE LIGHT WITHIN:

HOW I OVERCAME BLINDNESS

CHIDI E. IKPEAMAEZE

DEDICATION

This book is dedicated, first and foremost, to God Almighty, whose boundless grace, mercy, and unwavering guidance have been my anchor through every step of this journey. Without His strength, none of this would have been possible. To Him be all the glory for the inspiration behind this work.

To my fellow warriors—the resilient souls living with disabilities, and to those who devote their lives to caring for, supporting, and advocating for them. Your strength, perseverance, and unwavering spirit are a testament to the power of the human will. May this book serve as a reminder that your worth is immeasurable and your light unquenchable, no matter the challenges you face.

Finally, I dedicate this work to the Chidi Light Empowerment Foundation, a vision birthed from a deep desire to uplift and empower persons with disabilities. May it stand as a beacon of hope, offering support, opportunities, and a path toward a brighter future—not just in Nigeria, but across the world.

Table of Contents

DEDICATION ....

INTRODUCTION ....

Nnem, My Mother...

CHAPTER 1:.. 1

THE DAWN OF LIFE 1

My Father's Strength, My Mother's Grace 1
Childhood Experiences 4
The King of The Air 5
The Fall.. 6
The One and Only Fight of My Life: My Fight with the Bully Girl 7
A Principal's Son: Trapped in a Glass Cage 10
Shyness And Gentleness: Strength Or Weakness? 11

CHAPTER 2:...14

MY DEAR COUSIN, THE APPLE, AND MY EYES.......14

The Diagnoses 16
Breaking the News to My Family 19
The News Spread in The Community 23
I Gave Up, but My Family Didn't 24

CHAPTER 3:...27

MY FEARS AND PAIN 27

My Mother's Heart Attack 27
My Father's Prophetic Words Changed Everything for Me 28
Temporary Relief at My Maternal Home 30
Yet Another Strike 31
My Greatest Loss: My Grandma Died 31

CHAPTER 4:...34

OUR EXPERIENCES WITH 'SOLUTION PROVIDERS'
.... 34

A Fake Pastor scammed us 34
Felix: Brother By blood, Friend by Choice 35
The Journey to the River 36
The Final Night and Aftermath................................ 38
Victims of Deception.. 38
Seeking God beyond Healing 39
Mr. Ubong and his Medicine.................................... 40
The Journey Begins 42
The Cost of Hope: Fire in my Eyes 45
Dwindling Hope 46
Another Attempt at a Cure 46
Mr. Ndah, the 'Spirit-Stricken Impotent' Man.......... 47
The Solution and the Night of Reckoning 51
A Miraculous Arrival 55

CHAPTER 5: 58
COMING TO TERMS WITH BLINDNESS 58

The Role of My Faith.. 58
Gratitude: My Lifeline 59
Visions: Another Lifeline 61
The Word and Promises of God 62

CHAPTER 6: 65
THE LIGHT OF EDUCATION 65

Going Back to School as a Blind Man 66
Faith Becomes My Friend.. 68
My encounter with Braille 69
My First Classroom Experience as a Blind Person........................ 72
A Lesson in Perspective.. 75
My First Letter to Papa 76
I Graduated in Eight Months instead of Two Years 77

CHAPTER 7: 78
THE CALL THAT CHANGED EVERYTHING 78

Bethesda 82

My Night Dreams..84

CHAPTER 8: 91
MY JOURNEY TO THE UNIVERSITY AND BEYOND 91

Choosing Sociology: My Motivation and Experiences 94

My Ideology about Giving..96

Challenges during Lectures 97

Graduation and Reflection..98

CHAPTER 9: 100
MIRACULOUS ENCOUNTERS AND DIVINE
PROTECTION 100

A Miraculous Rescue: Saved by an Unseen Hand 102

A Brush with Disaster: The Miracle of an Intact Leg 104

The Pushing Bus and the Busy Road 105

Stranded on the Highway 106

CHAPTER 10: 110
MY FAMILY AND SIGNIFICANT RELATIONSHIPS 110

Relationships and Support Systems 112

Benjamin: My First and Truest friend 113

Christian: I Call Him Dodo 114

Bro Eze: The Kindest Man Ever 115

A Crush, a Trip, and a Painful Ankle 116

Sir Michael L: A Stranger's Kindness, A Father's Heart 118

The Blessing of Relationships..118

CHAPTER 11: 120
MY LOVE LIFE 120

Mary – My First Love 121

Adak: My Kind Friend. 122

The Pursuit of True Love 124

Then came my Joy 124

My relationship with Rayne..126

A Love That Wasn't Quite Love 129

A Lesson, Not a Lifelong Partner 133

CHAPTER 12: 135

BREAKING BARRIERS—MY FIRST JOB 135

CHAPTER 13: 137

CHIDI LIGHT EMPOWERMENT FOUNDATION FOR THE BLIND 137

The blind, the society, and my vision 137

CHAPTER 14: 140

WHY I SET UP THE GOFUNDME 140

CONCLUSION: 142

THE ROAD AHEAD: A PROMISE TO THE FUTURE 142

APPRECIATION 145

ABOUT THE AUTHOR 146

INTRODUCTION

There are two kinds of people I've come to discover in this life. The first are those for whom life seems effortless—those who have it handed to them on a silver platter, gliding through existence as if it were a bed of roses. Surrounded by fortunate circumstances and special privileges, they navigate life with ease, basking in comfort, growth, and countless blessings.

Then there are those whose journey tells a different story—a tale marked by shattered dreams and relentless struggles. They endure the storms of disappointment, the winds of disaster, and the tidal waves of grief that threaten to pull them under. Yet, even as they are battered by life's trials, they persevere, displaying a resilience that is nothing short of extraordinary.

I know this because I am one of them.

At the age of 17, I was diagnosed with glaucoma, and the inevitable news of blindness felt like a death sentence to my dreams and aspirations, forcing me to navigate a world I had never imagined. But this moment of profound loss marked the beginning of an extraordinary journey.

This autobiography chronicles my path from a carefree childhood to the day my world turned dark and beyond. It's a story of pain and fear, resilience and hope, fueled by unwavering faith. It is about finding the courage to triumph over the limitations that threatened to hold me back. Through the challenges and triumphs, it is God's mercy and grace that illuminated my path and gave me the strength to persevere.

Join me as I share the pivotal moments, the struggles, and the victories that have shaped who I am today. This is not just a story about blindness; it's about seeing the limitless possibilities within ourselves, acknowledging the undying love of a wonderful family, and recognizing the kindness of humanity, as well as the divine hand guiding us through adversity. It's a testament to the power of faith, resilience, and the extraordinary growth that comes from trusting in God's plan. I hope that my journey will inspire and encourage you to overcome your own adversities, recognizing that with faith, strength, and determination, we can all triumph over the challenges life throws our way

Nnem, My Mother

"As I sat beside my son in the doctor's office, the words "glaucoma" sounded so big and strange to me and didn't matter much until the doctor associated it with "impending blindness" Then it hit me like a bolt of lightning. My heart sank, and an intense wave of sorrow washed over me. Tears welled up in my eyes, but I fought to hold them back, knowing I needed to be strong for my son.

I couldn't believe what I was hearing. My mind raced to process the harsh reality that my vibrant, hopeful boy was going to lose his sight. The pain was almost unbearable—a deep ache in my chest that seemed to radiate through my entire being. Seeing the shock and fear etched on his face broke my heart even more.

A fierce protective instinct surged within me. I wanted to do anything and everything to take this burden away from him, to find some solution or miracle that the doctor hadn't mentioned. But as the doctor continued speaking, offering treatment options and reassurances, I felt a crushing sense of helplessness. How could I protect him from this? How could I make it better?

My mind swirled with worries about his future. How would he navigate life without sight? How would he cope with the loss of his independence, dreams, and plans? I felt an overwhelming burden of responsibility, knowing I had to support

him through this daunting journey, yet my own heart faltered under the weight. I struggled to bear it.

Time has passed, and I've come to see through his eyes. Chidi is a special child, and there is a strange, powerful light within him that continues to shine brightly"

'Mother'

Memory Lane

Chapter 1:
THE DAWN OF LIFE

April 4th, 1990—a day etched in my family's hearts, filled with boundless joy and overwhelming gratitude. The day I was born. My mother often recalls my birth as the easiest among her children, a memory she cherishes with fondness. "You were such a placid child," she'd say, her voice tinged with warmth. It was as if even then, I was destined to bring calm amidst the storm.

I am the fifth child of six children, born into a loving home deeply rooted in Igbo heritage. I hail from Mgbokor Okpulor, Obingwa, in Aba Ngwa, Abia State—a place rich in culture and history. My identity is woven into the vibrant traditions of my people, a legacy that has shaped my values, resilience, and the unwavering spirit with which I embrace life.

Healthy, whole, and without a single complication, I entered this world under the watchful eyes of the Almighty. Growing up, I remained extraordinarily healthy—mentally sharp, physically strong, and emotionally balanced. It felt as if nature itself conspired to favor me, a blessing I never took for granted.

My Father's Strength, My Mother's Grace

I grew up wrapped in the embrace of a loving family, nurtured by the unwavering strength of my parents.

My father was a paradox of a man—loving yet firm, caring yet unyielding, a man whose life had been shaped by hardship but defined by sheer determination.

He lost his parents early, a cruel twist of fate that left him and his siblings in the frail hands of their aging grandmother. She did what she could, but survival was a daily battle. With no guiding hand to smooth his path and no safety net to catch him when life pushed him down, he quickly learned that the world did not owe him kindness. Yet, instead of surrendering to despair, he gritted his teeth, squared his shoulders, and forged ahead with nothing but raw willpower and an unbreakable spirit.

While other children spent their days running barefoot through the fields, chasing dreams and butterflies, my father was busy chasing survival. He worked on farms, cut firewood, carried heavy loads—anything to scrape together enough to keep his dream of education alive. And though his journey was grueling, his brilliance refused to be dimmed. His academic excellence turned heads, earned him scholarships, and finally paved the way for a future beyond mere survival. When he became a teacher, he didn't just embrace the profession—he attacked it with the same fire that had fueled his rise from hardship to success.

But struggle leaves its imprint. My father had battled life and won, but the war had shaped him into a man of unwavering principles, discipline, and an intolerance for laziness. *"There is no food for the lazy,"* he often declared, his voice carrying the weight of someone who had once starved but refused to be defeated by it.

Determined that his children would never taste the bitterness of his past, he ran our household with the precision of a military drill instructor. Idleness was a crime. If you had time to sit, you had time to work. School was non-negotiable, but so was farm work. While other kids enjoyed carefree days, we juggled books with back-breaking labor. Holidays were not for rest; they were for tilling the land, planting crops, and weeding with ruthless efficiency.

And then there were his rules—strict, unwavering, and, at times, as unbendable as steel. Noise? Unacceptable. Wastage? A punishable offense. Carelessness? A cardinal sin. He had a radar for undone chores and misplaced items, and his discipline was swift and sometimes severe.

Yet beneath the iron exterior was a heart that loved deeply—a heart that had known suffering and only wanted to shield us from it. He wasn't just raising children; he was crafting warriors, molding us with the same fire that had refined him.

Of course, to a child, love wrapped in sternness doesn't always feel like love. And so, one day, in exasperation, my younger sister Blessing gave him a title we all secretly agreed was well-earned: *"Iron Bender."*

At the time, we laughed in whispers, careful not to let him hear. But today, I understand. My father was not just a disciplinarian; he was a protector, a sculptor chiseling strength, resilience, and purpose into us. He carried the scars of his struggles, but instead of letting them break him, he used them to build a foundation for us—one of unyielding faith, relentless hard work, and a determination that refused to be broken.

Yet, before my siblings and I were born, my parents faced a sorrow so deep it could have shattered them—they lost their first four children. It was a grief that could have drained the warmth from their hearts, but instead, it deepened their love, making every child who followed even more precious. Perhaps that pain was why my father fought so fiercely—to build a future where loss would not define us. And perhaps it is why my mother holds on to us with such tenderness, as if loving us fiercely could somehow bridge the gap between what she lost and what she still has.

My mother—the gentlest force of love and warmth in our home.

If my father was steel, she is the steady, calming breeze. If he was fire, she is water, tempering his edges and filling the spaces he left untouched.

She is beautiful, soft-spoken, the kindest, most selfless soul I have ever known. Her love is a quiet thing, woven into every act of service, every gentle word, every knowing glance that tells us she understands, even when we say nothing.

With her, our home is not just a place—it is a haven. She makes it warm, comfortable, a refuge from the world. We feel safe with her, knowing that no matter what the day brings, we can return to the unwavering embrace of her love. She is the one we can confide in, the one who listens without judgment, who soothes our fears with patience and wisdom.

She lives up to her name in every sense—peace-loving, enduring, filled with an unshakable grace that makes her presence feel like a constant prayer. And, indeed, she is a woman of prayer. She prays over us, for us, with us. Long before we understood the power of those whispered words, she was covering us with them, believing in the things we could not yet see.

It was her patience that softened the sharpness of my father's discipline. Her peace that balanced his authority. Her tenderness that reminded us that strength does not always have to be loud.

Together, they were the perfect paradox. My father gave us discipline, my mother gives us comfort. He pushed us forward, she catches us when we stumble. He prepared us for the world, she reminds us that, despite its hardships, there is still love, still grace, still a reason to hope.

I am who I am because of them both. And for that, I will always be grateful.

Childhood Experiences

Growing up, I was a bundle of strength and energy, a child as sturdy as an iroko tree and as agile as a cat leaping off a rooftop. And I owe much of this to my mother's legendary cooking. She didn't just feed us; she fortified us. Our staple diet was a feast fit for warriors—fufu, eba, pounded yam, all paired with fresh, steaming vegetable soups rich with flavors that could make even the weariest soul feel reborn. We devoured organic fruits and nuts like they were nature's own medicine, and in many ways, they were. They fueled our bodies, sharpened our minds, and ensured we hardly ever fell sick.

With such a diet, you would expect me to be a rough, battle-hardened village champion, quick to throw punches and settle scores with fists. But, ironically, for all my strength and stamina, I was as gentle as a summer breeze. I disliked trouble, steered clear of conflict, and had a deep-seated aversion to fights. If there was chaos brewing, I was the first to slip away unnoticed. Watching people fight made my stomach churn and the idea of being in one myself? Absolutely horrifying.

Yet, despite my commitment to peace, life has a funny way of testing even the gentlest of souls. And so, there was one fateful day—the one and only time—I found myself in a fight. It was an experience so unexpected, so unforgettable, that to this day, it remains etched in my memory like a stubborn stain on a white garment. And trust me, this is a tale you simply must hear!

The King of The Air

We lived in a rural paradise, where towering trees stood like ancient guardians, their branches heavy with fruit and ripe for adventure. For me, those trees weren't just part of the scenery; they were my playground, my kingdom, my stairway to the skies. Climbing wasn't just a hobby—it was a calling. If there was a tree, I had to climb it. If it had fruit, I had to taste it.

Lucky for me, my two older brothers had no love for climbing. Whether it was fear, laziness, or simply a lack of ambition, they left the treetops to me. And oh, what a privilege it was! The entire orchard was mine to conquer. If anyone in the family wanted fresh mangoes, guavas, or oranges, they had to come to me—the undisputed ruler of the branches. I was the gatekeeper of nature's bounty, the self-appointed minister of fruit distribution, and let's be honest, I sometimes taxed my subjects—a mango here, a guava there—before handing over their requested share.

I wasn't just good at climbing; I was exceptional. No tree was too tall, no branch too tricky. While others hesitated at the sight of a towering iroko or a wobbly palm tree, I saw a challenge, a dare from nature itself. I would scale up effortlessly, defying gravity with the grace of a monkey and the confidence of a champion. Up there, high above the ground, with the wind whistling through my ears, I felt invincible. I was the King of the Air, surveying my leafy domain from my throne of branches, ruling with pride and—let's be honest—a bit of mischief.

Looking back, those trees taught me more than just how to climb. They taught me courage, strategy, and the art of perseverance. They showed me that reaching for greater heights—whether in a tree or in life—takes a mix of confidence, skill, and a little bit of madness. And most importantly, they taught me that when you're the only one willing to go higher, you get to enjoy the sweetest fruits first.

The Fall

Even kings have their downfalls—sometimes quite literally. And on one unforgettable afternoon, the King of the Air learned this the hard way.

It all started innocently enough. A woman in our compound, impressed by my tree-climbing prowess, asked me to pluck some fruits from her backyard tree. Of course, I accepted the mission with the confidence of a seasoned warrior going into battle. I had conquered mightier trees before—what was one more? With my usual grace, I ascended, each step a testament to my mastery. The higher I went, the prouder I felt, my hands and feet moving with the precision of an expert.

But pride, as they say, comes before a fall.

At the very top, I made a grave mistake—I stepped onto a dry branch, thin and brittle, its loyalty to the tree long gone. The moment my weight pressed down, it gave way with a loud snap, and in an instant, my throne betrayed me. Down I plummeted, crashing through layers of branches, leaves whipping against my skin, gravity pulling me with an unforgiving grip.

Below, the woman let out a scream so loud, I'm sure the entire neighborhood heard. She must have imagined the worst—bones shattering, blood spilling, the tragic fall of a once-great climber. But fate had other plans. By some miracle, I landed on my feet—shaken, scratched, but intact. I stood there, breathless, processing the sheer absurdity of what had just happened.

The woman, trembling with shock, rushed to me, grabbing me as if to confirm that I was still in one piece. Her hands were shaking more than mine. For a moment, we just stood there—her holding onto me, me standing like a resurrected ghost, both of us trying to make sense of it.

That day, I learned an important lesson—one that went far beyond tree climbing. Life, like a tree, offers moments of triumph and peril. No matter how skilled, strong, or confident you are, there will always be unexpected falls. Branches will break. Gravity will remind you that you are not invincible. But here's the secret: it's not about never falling; it's about how you land. Some falls will bruise you, humble you, shake you to your core. But if you land on your feet—if you rise despite the drop—you've already won.

From that day on, I never took any branch for granted, no matter how strong it looked. And in life, I learned to always test my footing before taking the next step because, sometimes, the greatest lessons don't come from climbing high, but from falling and standing tall again.

The One and Only Fight of My Life: My Fight with the Bully Girl

Now, let me take you back to my junior secondary school days—an era when my biggest worry wasn't exams or assignments but a certain girl whose fists had earned her the reputation of a schoolyard tyrant.

She wasn't just any bully. No, she was a force of nature—strong, confident, and terrifyingly fearless. Unlike the typical bullies who targeted the weak, she had a peculiar hobby: beating up boys; and not just any boys, but the ones who were supposed to be strong and untouchable in our socio-cultural setting. You see, where I grew up, a boy getting beaten up by a girl was a disgrace of legendary proportions. If such a tragedy befell you, you wouldn't just lose respect—you'd become the subject of endless jokes, songs, and exaggerated tales that would follow you for life.

One fateful afternoon, during the break, my classmates and I, including the infamous bully, sat together, sharing jokes and banter. Now, I can't recall exactly what I said to her—it must have been something innocent, or so I thought—but she took offense. In an instant, her face twisted in fury, and before I knew it, she was unleashing a barrage of insults at me, her voice sharp enough to slice through metal.

I chose the path of peace. I kept my mouth shut and endured her verbal onslaught. But my so-called friends? Oh, they weren't having it. They turned against me, mocking me relentlessly. "Ah-ah, so you will just stand there and take that?" *"Are you a man or a mannequin?"* *"Even a wall would talk back!"*

The pressure was unbearable. I wanted to disappear. So, with my pride hanging by a thread, I did the only thing I could—I walked away. And not just any walk. It was the slow, defeated kind, head low, eyes burning with unshed tears.

Later that day, I saw her alone in a more secluded area. It was my chance—not to fight, but to reason with her, to let her know that her words had stung and that I didn't appreciate them. Maybe, just maybe, I could appeal to her better nature.

But life, as I have come to learn, often has different plans.

Just as I was trying to express myself, my ever-loyal friends—yes, the same ones who had mocked me earlier—spotted us and sprinted over. Their eyes gleamed with excitement. They weren't here to play peacemakers. No, they had come for entertainment. A fight was brewing, and they wanted front-row seats.

And that's when she made her move.

Without warning, she charged at me like a wrestler in the final round. Her plan was clear—lift me off my feet and slam me to the ground, publicly shattering whatever was left of my dignity.

In that split second, I saw my future flash before my eyes: the endless humiliation, the laughter, the retelling of my downfall for generations to come. I knew that if I let her execute her plan, my life as I knew it would be over.

So, I did something I never thought I would do.

I abandoned all principles of nonviolence, threw away my peace-loving nature, and with all the desperation of a cornered prey, I swung my fist.

The impact was immediate. She staggered back, clutching her nose as blood trickled down. The air fell silent. Even my friends, the instigators, looked stunned. She fell to the ground, sobbing loudly.

I stood there, frozen. Horror gripped me. What had I done? I, the boy who detested violence, had just punched someone. And not just anyone—a girl!

Before I could even process my actions, we were dragged to the school authorities. Justice was swift and merciless. I was punished severely—not just because of the fight, but because my father was the principal. The moment I stepped into his office, I knew I was doomed.

That day, I learned a valuable lesson. Sometimes, life puts us in situations where we must defend ourselves, but violence—no matter how justified it seems—often comes with consequences we may not be prepared for.

From that day forward, I made a vow: Never again would I raise my fists in anger. Never again would I let others dictate my reactions. And most importantly, never again would I underestimate the unpredictable twists of life.

After all, in the grand game of life, wisdom is the greatest weapon.

A Principal's Son: Trapped in a Glass Cage

Please, whatever you do, don't let my father know about this. Actually, on second thought, go ahead—tell him. The man was well-intentioned, and I'll forever be grateful for his love, both the kind that hugged me tight and the kind that straightened me out. After all, every sculptor needs a chisel, and all his efforts helped shape this masterpiece called 'Chidi.'

Growing up, I had what many might consider a "privileged" education—I attended both primary and secondary school under the rule of a principal who was not just the head of the school but also the head of my household. Yes, my father. Now, let me tell you, this wasn't the academic jackpot you might think it was.

While other kids strolled through school, carefree and unnoticed, I walked around feeling like a fish in a very, very transparent bowl. Every move I made, every word I uttered, every breath I took—it all seemed to be under a giant magnifying glass. Any small mistake on my part would trigger gasps, whispers, and the dreaded statement: "Even you? The son of the principal?" Oh, the horror!

It felt as though I had unknowingly signed up for a lifetime membership to the "Model Student Association"—an organization where failure was not an option, and discipline was dished out with the precision of a Swiss watch. Other students could get away with minor mischief. They could be noisy, sneak snacks into class, or conveniently "forget" their homework. Me? The moment I even sneezed too loudly, it became headline news.

To make matters worse, my father was not just *any* principal—he was the no-nonsense, iron-fisted, rules-are-rules type. His reputation for discipline struck fear into the hearts of students far and wide, and unfortunately for me, that fear had side effects. Since they couldn't dare challenge him directly, they did the next best thing—they took out their frustrations on me and my younger sister, Blessing.

If I so much as breathed in the wrong direction, my father wouldn't hesitate to make an example of me. And by "example," I don't mean a gentle reminder or a slap on the wrist. No, he would deliver a full-scale, no-mercy disciplinary session right there at school—a public demonstration of fairness that left other students trembling in their shoes. If the principal's own son wasn't spared, what hope did they have?

Was it a great school? Yes. Did I love it? Not exactly. It's hard to enjoy a place where your every move feels like an audition for sainthood. Looking back, though, I realize my father wasn't just raising a student—he was raising a man. A man who, despite feeling like a walking cautionary tale, learned resilience, discipline, and the importance of integrity.

Still, let's be honest—if given a choice, I would have happily traded places with any random student whose biggest worry was finishing their lunch before the break ended.

Shyness And Gentleness: Strength Or Weakness?

I have always been a very shy person—and, to be honest, I still am. Crowds? No, thank you! From a young age, I found public attention overwhelming. One of my earliest memories of this was in kindergarten when I was given a special song or memory verse to present in church. The moment I stepped to the front, my tiny hands trembling, I would bury my face in the hymn book, pretending to study the lyrics with great intensity—not because I didn't know the words, but because I was too shy to look up. The congregation always found it amusing, and laughter would ripple through the church whenever I was called to sing or recite.

This aversion to the spotlight wasn't limited to church. In school, I had an unspoken rule: the front row was enemy territory. I instinctively gravitated to the back of the classroom, where I could blend in like a shadow. The same went for church—sitting anywhere near the front felt like voluntarily placing myself under a giant spotlight.

But perhaps my shyness reached its peak at home. Whenever relatives visited, instead of rushing to greet them like a well-mannered child, I executed my classic disappearing act— diving under the bed and staying there until the coast was clear. It wasn't that I didn't like them; I just dreaded the attention that came with the usual greetings and small talk.

Looking back, I realize that my shyness shaped much of who I am. While it kept me out of trouble, it also meant I often went unnoticed. But here's the irony—sometimes, the quietest voices have the loudest impact. And perhaps, in my own way, I was simply saving my words for the right moments.

However, life has a way of teaching us that staying in the background forever isn't an option. I came to understand that courage isn't the absence of fear—it's taking a step forward despite it. I learned that boldness doesn't always mean being the loudest in the room; sometimes, it means daring to be heard when it truly matters. And so, little by little, I embraced the challenge of stepping out, of owning my space, of realizing that my voice, too, deserved to be heard.

But make no mistake—shyness is one of the things I must conquer. If you, like me, have ever shrunk back from speaking up, let me tell you: don't be like me. Square your shoulders, look life in the face, and express yourself. The world won't know what you have to offer if you keep hiding under the bed!

✦ ✦ ✦ ✦ ✦✦ ✦ ✦

Blindness

✦ ✦ ✦ ✦ ✦✦ ✦ ✦

Chapter 2:
MY DEAR COUSIN, THE APPLE, AND MY EYES

To me, being sixteen was like being a star shot straight into the heavens—limitless, full of light, and unstoppable. As a young man with most of my life ahead of me, I embraced every moment like it was a Christmas gift, beautifully presented on a golden platter. I was a bright student, always bouncing between first and second position in class, fueled by my passion for science. My dream? To study metallurgical engineering and become a top-tier engineer.

I had big, passionate dreams, brimming with ambition. With these lofty visions, I hit the road of life, fully expecting smooth highways and clear skies ahead. But how could I have known about the rocky bends and unexpected detours? Living in a world so unpredictable, how could I foresee the lessons that only experience—life's toughest teacher—could offer? Sadly, this teacher was waiting to deliver its lessons the hard and bitter way.

My hard lesson began on May 20th, 2006, when I was in Junior Secondary 3 at the age of 16. This bleak and dark day will forever live in my memory. It all began on a sunny and hot Monday afternoon when my cousin and I returned from school. We were the same age, in the same class, and childhood friends who shared many things in common. Hardly could you see one of us apart from the other. Due to our closeness, some people even described us as twins.

That fateful afternoon, a tragic mishap struck that altered the course of our friendship and our lives. As always, we sought each other's companionship and assistance whenever we had something to do. My cousin came over to our house and asked for my help. An aunt had sent him to pluck some fruits from a tree in their backyard. We locally call the fruit rose apple or bell apple—it has a bell-like shape, smooth red or pink skin, and soft, white, juicy flesh. Because of its tenderness, the fruit would spoil if it hit the ground. So, he needed someone to stand below and catch them while he climbed the tree to pluck them.

Though I was hungry and tired, I couldn't say no to my dear cousin and friend. I readily obliged and went with him. As we walked the short distance to his backyard, I had no idea I was about to learn one of the toughest and hardest lessons of my life. When we arrived, he climbed the tree and began plucking the fruits while I stood on the ground, catching them. It was a smooth and interesting task until, suddenly, an accidental apple fell from the branch and hit me in the right eye.

The impact was so intense that I was thrown to the ground. The only thing I remember is lying on the ground, crying and rolling in pain. The pain was so excruciating that I lost all sense of my surroundings. Before my cousin could climb down from the tree, others who heard my sharp cry had already surrounded me. They immediately took me home.

My eye was swollen and red, forming lumps of blood. My parents were shocked and devastated when they saw my condition. It had been only a few minutes since I left the house. Without asking many questions, they quickly took me to a local chemist where we usually got prescriptions. The chemist gave me eye drops and some other medications.

When we returned home, applying the eye drops and taking the other medications provided great relief from the pain. I slept comfortably that night, and within three days of consistent use of the eye drops, the thick blood around my eyeball cleared. It was as if my eyeball had been washed with soap and water, returning to its normal color. Life continued as usual.

However, a year later, at the age of 17, I began noticing some worrying abnormalities in my sight. I struggled to see clearly what was written on the blackboard if I was sitting at the back; everything looked blurry unless I moved to the front. Another abnormality was that each time we went to the farm, after bending down to dig the ridges, it seemed as if there was dew everywhere when I stood up. These abnormalities caused me deep concern after observing them for some time. I didn't hesitate; I told my parents about my experiences. They were understandably worried and scared. The next day, my mother took me to the hospital, where a doctor examined my eyes.

The Diagnoses

As we sat in the hospital reception, waiting for the doctor's verdict, time stretched unbearably. Each second felt like an hour, each breath a struggle against the growing dread in my chest. My mother sat beside me, wringing her hands, her lips moving in silent prayer. I tried to steady my racing thoughts, but they crashed against my mind like storm-tossed waves.

What if it was nothing serious? Perhaps it was just a minor infection, something a few pills or eye drops could fix. But then, why did the doctor take so long? Why had the nurse given me that look—the one that made my stomach sink?

When we were finally called into the office, the tension thickened. The doctor sat behind his desk, his expression unreadable, flipping through my file with an unsettling silence. Beside him, the nurse stood stiffly, her face a careful mask. I studied them both, searching for clues, for anything that could hint at good news. But there was none.

Then came the first blow.

"Does blindness run in your family?" the doctor asked, his voice steady but weighted with something ominous.

My mother stiffened beside me, blinking rapidly as if trying to process the question. *"No,"* she answered, barely above a whisper. *"No one. No one in our family has ever been blind."*

The doctor nodded, his gaze flickering between us. He turned to me. *"Tell me again—when did you first notice changes in your vision?"*

I recounted everything: the trouble reading the blackboard, the strange mist that clouded my vision after bending down on the farm, and the little things that seemed insignificant at first but had gradually worsened.

The doctor listened without interrupting. When I finished, he leaned back in his chair, sighing heavily. He looked at my mother again, his next words laced with quiet reproach. *"Why did you wait this long to bring him in?"*

My mother flinched as if struck. *"We... we only just noticed,"* she stammered, her voice breaking.

The doctor remained silent for a moment, his fingers tapping against his desk. Then, in an unexpected turn, he asked, "Do you know Helen Keller?"

I blinked. "No."

"What about Stevie Wonder?" "Not really, but my father used to tell us about them. Blind folks,

Again, I shook my head. My frustration flared. Why was he asking me about blind people when all I wanted was a solution?

The doctor exhaled, rubbing his forehead as if debating how best to break the news. Then, with measured words, he spoke:

"You have glaucoma."

The room fell silent.

The words didn't register at first. Glaucoma. It sounded foreign, like the name of a distant country, something irrelevant to my reality.

But then he continued.

"There's very little we can do."

A heavy weight settled in my stomach. My fingers curled around the edge of the chair, my knuckles turning white.

"With the equipment we have here, the most we can do is manage it. For real treatment, you'd need advanced medical care—perhaps in India." He paused, hesitating before adding, "Otherwise... eventually, you will lose your sight."

Shock overwhelmed me, a chilling wave of disbelief that left me numb. My heart pounded in my chest, and my breath caught in my throat as if the air had become too heavy to inhale. The room seemed to tilt, and for a moment, I felt disconnected

17

from reality, unable to believe that this devastating news could be about me. Blind? At 17?

Pain, sharp and visceral, soon followed. It wasn't just a physical ache but a deep emotional wound that cut through my very being. I thought of all my dreams and plans—graduating, traveling, pursuing my passions—all now overshadowed by the impending darkness. The future I had envisioned crumbled before my eyes, replaced by a bleak, uncertain void. Tears welled up, stinging my eyes as I struggled to maintain composure, yet the sense of loss was overwhelming.

Fear soon took hold, an all-encompassing dread that gripped my heart and refused to let go. Questions bombarded my mind: How will I live without sight? What will become of my independence? Who will I be in a world plunged into darkness? The unknown loomed large and terrifying, a chasm of uncertainty pulling me inexorably.

My hands trembled as I clutched the edge of the consulting table, seeking stability in a world that had suddenly become unstable and threatening. Every aspect of my life— school, friends, family—flashed before me, and the prospect of navigating it all without vision seemed insurmountable. The fear of becoming a burden, of losing my identity and ability to contribute meaningfully, gnawed at my spirit.

The doctor's voice became a distant murmur, offering reassurances and encouragement that barely scratched the surface of my despair. My dreams of becoming an engineer, my ambitions, my independence—all of it blurred, fading into an uncertain, terrifying darkness.

I wanted to scream, to protest, and to demand a different answer. But there was none. And for the first time, I understood what it meant to feel truly helpless.

I turned to my mother, and what I saw shattered me completely. Tears streamed down her face, her body trembling with silent sobs. She clutched her chest as if trying to hold in the pain, but it was spilling out, raw and uncontrollable.

And that was when it hit me—this wasn't just about me; It was about her too. A woman who had already lost five children. A woman who had fought to keep me alive, only to now be told that her bright, ambitious son was going blind. I feared she was teetering on the edge of that abyss once more, drowning in a grief too deep for words.

Pain speaks in many accents, but my mother's anguish was one I knew too well. As crushing as the diagnosis was, nothing tore me apart more than seeing her like this. Despite my own despair, I knew I had to hold myself together—for her sake. I needed to get her home.

In the end, the doctor made it clear: we had to prepare for a trip to India for advanced ophthalmological diagnosis. Their limited equipment couldn't conduct all the necessary tests and examinations. After hearing everything the doctor had to say, we left the hospital and began the painful journey home—wrapped in silence, drowning in tears. I was in shock, not just from the diagnosis of glaucoma, but from the helplessness in the doctor's voice. The weight of it all bore down on me, but the real blow came when I thought about what lay ahead—the impossible cost of traveling abroad for treatment. I knew, with painful certainty, that my family simply couldn't afford it. Even now, I struggle to understand how my vision could have deteriorated so drastically in just a single year—without a warning, without a sign.

Breaking the News to My Family

When we got back home, everyone was anxious to hear what the doctor had said. My eye issue had become a major concern for everyone, but no one had anticipated that it had escalated to the extent we were told at the hospital.

As soon as we stepped into the house, my mother's tears overflowed, breaking the sad news to everyone without her needing to say a word. Her face was contorted with grief, and her sobs echoed through the silence. My siblings gathered around, looking at each other with worry, their faces pale with fear and uncertainty.

The atmosphere was heavy with sorrow and agony, as if a dark cloud had descended upon our home. It felt like a death had occurred—not just of sight, but of dreams and aspirations. The weight of the diagnosis pressed down on everyone, leaving us suffocated by despair.

Amid this, my father—the pillar of strength and stern discipline—broke down. Seeing him cry was a shock and a great devastation. He had always been the unyielding rock, the one who held us all together with his strength and resolve. But now, his tears flowed freely, showing the profound grief and helplessness he felt. His sobs were silent but deep, each tear symbolizing his shattered hopes for me and the reminder of his financial incapability.

His vulnerability in that moment mirrored the anguish that engulfed us all. We stood together, enveloped in a sorrowful embrace, our collective pain forging an unspoken bond of shared grief and love.

The sorrow in the room was almost tangible, the air thick with unspoken fears and the weight of an uncertain future. Each of us struggled to find solace in one another, but the news was too heavy to bear. It felt like a profound loss—not just of my sight, but of the carefree days we once knew.

As I sat in silence, listening to the muffled cries of my family, I realized this wasn't just my battle—it was ours. And no matter how dark the road ahead seemed, I wasn't walking it alone.

This was the first time I had ever seen my father cry. And I knew—it wasn't just because I would likely lose my sight. He cried because the only solution was beyond his reach. He couldn't afford a medical trip to India, and there was no one to turn to, no help in sight. We were in the village, surrounded by limited information, opportunities, and possibilities. This helplessness—this burden—was one he carried until his very last breath.

Years later, in December 2016, I would come to understand just how deeply he carried it.

At the time, I was still studying at UNILAG but had traveled home to Aba for Christmas. I had gone to visit my oldest sister, Mercy when we received news that my father had fallen ill and was hospitalized. On December 26th, Mercy, her family, and I went to see our parents at the hospital. My sister Victoria had also made the journey from Port Harcourt to be there.

We spent the entire day by our father's bedside—talking, watching over him, keeping our mother company. None of us could have known how significant that day would become.

By evening, it was time to leave.

Mercy, her family and I left first, while Victoria stayed behind a little longer. Later, she shared a story with us—one that has never left my heart.

She told us:

I was set to leave—to travel back to Port Harcourt—because work was waiting for me the next day. I had picked up my purse, said my goodbyes, and was ready to walk out the door.

But then, my mother's voice stopped me in my tracks.

It wasn't just what she said—it was how she said it. There was a weight in her tone, a desperation I had never heard before.

"Chai! Are you going to leave me all alone? Please don't go. Please stay with me tonight."

I turned to her, and in that moment, I truly saw her. Not just as my mother, but as a woman on the edge of something unbearable. Her voice trembled with a fear she wasn't used to showing, a loneliness she could already feel creeping in.

I didn't think twice. I dropped my purse and nodded.

"I'll stay."

It didn't matter that I had no change of clothes. It didn't matter that I hadn't planned to sleep over. The relief in her eyes made every inconvenience meaningless.

That night, she stepped into the bathroom to freshen up, leaving me alone with my father. The room was dim and unusually silent and sad. I sat beside him, watching his frail body rise and fall with each labored breath.

Then, he stirred.

His eyelids fluttered, and I could see the effort it took just to lift them. He wanted to speak.

I helped him sit up, supporting his frail frame as best as I could. His eyes, sunken yet still filled with something unspoken, found mine.

His voice was weak, each word a battle against the exhaustion pulling him under. But he spoke anyway—because he had to.

"Umunne gi alala we?" (Have your siblings gone?)

I swallowed hard and nodded. "Yes, sir."

He let out a slow breath, and then, with the last remnants of his strength, he called my name.

"Victoria."

There was something in the way he said it—tender, heavy, final. I felt it in my chest, a sharp, sinking feeling. I adjusted his pillow, trying to make him comfortable.

He waited a moment, then, as if summoning every ounce of life he had left, he spoke again. His words were slow. Deliberate. Absolute.

"Biko, anya Chidia, unu agbadala ya nala. Mgbe obula uwa ngara unu, ganu uka anya ahu."

(It's about Chidi's eye condition. Please, you and your siblings must never give up on it. Whenever you are financially capable, seek a solution for Chidi's vision. Please, my daughter.)

My throat tightened. I forced a smile. "Okay, sir. We will definitely do that."

I didn't want to keep him talking—it was getting harder for him to breathe, and fear began to creep into my chest. His breaths grew more uneven. I called the nurses.

By then my mother had come out of the bathroom, and we helped him lie back down. His breathing slowed. Then it evened out. My mother and I sighed in relief, thinking he had finally found some rest.

But when the nurses arrived, they didn't find rest.

They found stillness.

And at that moment, as my mother crumpled beside him in grief, I realized how close I had come to leaving her to face this alone.

I was overwhelmingly grateful that she had asked me to stay"

"Victoria"

The News Spread in The Community

We didn't know how the news of my ordeal spread so quickly. The people who heard about it couldn't believe their ears. Many were shocked because they hadn't even known I was having an eye issue, especially since I was still seeing well at that time. This discrepancy between what I was experiencing and the reality of my condition was profoundly confusing. On one hand, I could still see relatively well, recognize people, move around freely, and handle most tasks myself, except for reading small letters. On the other hand, I had been told at the hospital that my eyes had deteriorated beyond remedy. The fact that I could still see, in terms of recognizing people and performing daily activities, provided me with a sense of hope and somewhat shielded me from the full impact of the harsh reality.

Previously, I had only seen elderly blind people, often accompanied by their grandchildren to church. I had never encountered anyone my age in such a condition, nor did I believe it was possible. But my own daunting experience was teaching me how wrong I had been.

Neighbors, friends, relatives, well-wishers, and others, from near and far, kept arriving in shock, expressing their sympathy, and offering their prayers and words of encouragement. As the calls and visits poured in, so did a multitude of recommendations for other places where we might find a solution.

I Gave Up, but My Family Didn't

As a family of faith, we believed in God's power to heal and perform miracles. Hope was the one thing we couldn't afford to lose. Clinging to that hope, we continued visiting various hospitals, searching desperately for a solution.

But with each visit, my pain deepened—not just because of the negative responses from doctors, but because of the financial strain it placed on my family. Eventually, my father had to start selling some of our properties to fund this desperate search for a cure. Yet, no matter how much we sacrificed, the answer remained the same.

One incident, in particular, made me swear never to step into another hospital again. We visited a high-profile medical center, and after a series of tests, the doctor suggested surgery—an attempt to salvage what remained of my sight. Though I already felt defeated, his next words struck me like a thunderbolt.

First, he warned us that if the surgery failed, I could lose my vision completely. But what came next shattered me even more—regardless of the surgery's outcome, I would experience ongoing pain and would need to remain on medication for life.

At that moment, something in me broke. How was I supposed to live with such a reality? Despair gripped me, and I gave up on hospitals altogether.

But while I lost hope, my family refused to.

Keep This:
Life often takes us through valleys of uncertainty, where hope feels distant and the weight of impossibility crushes our spirit. But even in those moments, we are never truly alone. The love and faith of those around us become a light, guiding us forward when we can't see the way. Strength is not just in fighting battles

24

but in knowing when to lean on those who walk beside us. Even when answers seem out of reach, resilience and faith can carry us through the darkest nights.

✦ ✦ ✦✦ ✦ ✦ ✦ ✦

The Trauma

✦ ✦ ✦ ✦ ✦✦ ✦ ✦

Chapter 3:
MY FEARS AND PAIN

As a young boy with my whole life ahead of me, I constantly wondered how I would cope with the ordeal of blindness and what it meant for my future. This was a reality I had neither foreseen nor prepared for, and words cannot truly capture how helpless I felt in the face of such an unpredictable, bleak circumstance.

As it became clear that the medical solution we desperately sought was beyond our reach, we were devastated. The financial burden of traveling overseas for examinations and possible treatment, as suggested by some of the doctors we had visited, was simply unattainable. Fear consumed me. I bitterly contemplated the future, seeing my education as an impossible dream. Life felt profoundly unfair.

During those days, I couldn't eat—food tasted bitter, like poison in my blood. I was broken and shattered, my days filled with suffocating anxiety and my nights darker than a thousand midnights. It felt as though my world had come to an abrupt and merciless end.

My Mother's Heart Attack

Amidst the colossal disappointment, my mother's emotional health deteriorated daily. She couldn't sleep at night and hardly ate her meals. In fact, tears became her sustenance. Each time she looked at me, her tears would start rolling down like a flowing stream. Her constant grief was so overwhelming that it sometimes felt even more debilitating than the eye condition itself. Her sorrow seemed to seep into every corner of our home, amplifying the heaviness of our shared pain.

I remember one night when I was sleeping in my room and suddenly heard a scream. It was my mother, who had run from the bed where she was sleeping with my father to the living room, struggling to breathe. She was having a heart attack.

The situation became so distressing that my uncle and grandmother decided to step in. They offered to take me in to live with them for a while, driven by their concern for both my well-being and my mother's deteriorating emotional state. My presence, though unintentional, seemed to exacerbate her suffering, and they recognized that her grief was becoming increasingly severe.

The prospect of leaving home brought me a significant sense of relief. It meant that I would no longer have to witness the daily heartache etched on my mother's face—a sight that was profoundly distressing for me. I hoped that by removing myself from the immediate environment, I could alleviate some of the emotional burden she was enduring.

In the end, this arrangement proved beneficial for both of us. Being with my uncle and grandmother provided me with a temporary escape from the relentless grief at home and gave my mother the space and time she needed to begin healing. The separation, though painful, allowed us both to cope with the situation in a healthier way.

My Father's Prophetic Words Changed Everything for Me

That painful night, as my mother's condition stabilized by God's grace, I remained in my room, overwhelmed by the intensity of the day. Through the thin walls, I could hear my father's voice, hushed and comforting, as he consoled my mother. His words, though tender, carried a weight that seemed to shift the atmosphere in our home.

In the quiet of that night, my father spoke words that would forever etch themselves into my heart. He said to her, "It is possible God allowed this ordeal to befall our son so He can lift and carry him to heights and levels in life he couldn't have reached with sight." His voice, though tinged with sorrow, was imbued with profound hope and faith. He suggested that perhaps this suffering had a higher purpose, that it could be the catalyst for something greater and more profound.

As I lay there, absorbing the resonance of his words, something transformative occurred within me. It was as if a glimmer of light had pierced through the darkness enveloping my spirit. For the first time in what felt like an eternity, I experienced a profound sense of relief. The crushing weight of despair seemed to lighten, and a spark of hope began to ignite within my soul.

My father's prophetic words were not mere consolation; they were a lifeline. They spoke of a purpose beyond the immediate pain, offering a perspective that saw potential within adversity. His belief that this struggle could be a stepping stone to greater heights resonated deeply with me. It was as if his faith was a bridge, leading me from the abyss of my fears to a place of renewed hope and possibility.

From that night forward, my orientation began to shift. The anguish that had once seemed insurmountable started to transform into a challenge I could confront with a sense of purpose. My father's words became a guiding light, illuminating a path through the darkness. They inspired resilience within me, a determination to seek the greater good in what seemed like an insurmountable obstacle.

In the face of such profound adversity, his words did more than offer solace—they redefined my reality. They planted a seed of belief that this struggle was not just a trial to endure but a journey toward something greater. My father's unwavering faith in the possibility of positive outcomes became a cornerstone of my own belief system, shaping the way I approached my challenges and setbacks.

Temporary Relief at My Maternal Home

Arriving at my maternal home, I felt happy again. My cousins, who were very fond of me, surrounded me with warmth and joy. Though they were troubled by my condition, they always found ways to cheer me up and help me momentarily forget my ordeal.

My grandmother—may her soul rest in peace—along with my uncle, his wife, and their children, knew exactly how to make me feel special. Their love and care turned my time with them into a rich and rewarding experience.

My grandmother was a strong, courageous, and kind woman. She was always there for me, and I cherished every moment with her. Everyone in that home adored me, making sure I was included in everything. My cousins never let me feel alone—they took me everywhere, proudly introducing me to their friends, who, in turn, became fond of me as well.

While at my maternal home, my grandmother took me to different places in search of a healing solution, but all efforts were in vain. By this time, my sight was deteriorating rapidly. Though I could still move around on my own, I struggled to see far distances and found it difficult to walk alone at night. My movement became limited, and my grandmother and uncle were always worried whenever I went out. They felt more at ease when I was with my cousins, knowing how much I loved to explore.

Even before my vision declined, walking around had always been one of my greatest joys. Now, as my world grew dimmer, my family became increasingly cautious. Though they never outright forbade me from moving around, their concern was evident—they simply wanted to keep me safe.

Yet Another Strike

While I sincerely understood my uncle's and grandmother's concerns and wisely limited my movements, I never anticipated the calamity that would ultimately shake the foundation of my hope and faith.

One gloomy evening, my failing vision betrayed me—I misjudged my surroundings, collided with a desk, and fell, striking my left eye on its sharp edge. A sharp pain shot through me, followed by a warm rush of blood. As I lay there, crying bitterly, my cousins rushed to my side. But when they saw the thick blood saturating my eye, their panic turned to tears. My grandmother was so distraught that she nearly fainted.

I was rushed to the hospital, where the doctor treated my injury. Then came the devastating news—my left eye had sustained severe damage. The words hit me like a hammer: both of my eyes were now critically affected, and my vision was slipping away faster than I had feared.

As I grieved, the love and care from my grandma and uncle's family were overwhelming. I begged them not to let my mother know about this, as I knew it would devastate her, and they agreed, understanding how fragile her emotions were. During this time, she visited with my father. When they saw the condition of my sight and realized I couldn't see as well as before, their hearts broke, and they wept bitterly. They wanted to take me back home with them, but my grandma and uncle refused, which I appreciated.

My Greatest Loss: My Grandma Died

As I grappled with the rapid decline of my precious sight, I thought I had reached the end of my suffering. But I was wrong, as another tragedy was about to strike that would almost take my life. One fateful day, after dinner with my grandmother, I went out with my cousin to buy some items. When we returned and were about to step into the house, we noticed that the whole family had gathered in the living room. We wondered what could have happened.

Immediately, we rushed into the house. To our horror, it was my dear grandmother sitting there writhing in pain. I wondered what could have gone wrong since it hadn't been ten minutes since we left the house. When I asked my uncle about the problem, he explained that she was suffering from bowel obstruction.

I tried talking to her, but the pain was so excruciating that she couldn't speak much. We were all confused and terrified. She was rushed to the hospital, and little did I know that night would be the last time I would ever speak to my precious grandma. The next morning, after all the necessary diagnoses, surgery was performed, but my grandmother did not survive.

I was traumatized and devastated. I felt as though my spirit had left me. I began to wonder why life was so hard on me. The pain I felt from the two accidents that struck my eyes was nothing compared to the grief I felt at the regrettable loss of my wonderful grandmother. Her absence created a vast vacuum in my life, overwhelming me with a profound sense of emptiness.

After her burial, I fell terribly ill due to grief, and my condition did not improve. My parents had to come and take me back home with them, and I remained sick for a long time. It was as if my whole world had come to an end.

From Despair to Hope

Amid all these trials and the constant fear of blindness, I kept praying and asking God for a way out. This period of intense suffering, loss, and emotional turmoil was an essential part of my journey, teaching me resilience and faith. It was in these dark moments that I began to see the faint glimmers of hope and strength that would guide me through the hardships of blindness.

The support of my family, the love they showed me during the darkest times, and the faith that slowly began to rekindle within me became the bedrock of my recovery. Even in the depths of despair, I found a flicker of light that encouraged me to keep moving forward, to believe that my life still had a purpose and that I could overcome the challenges that seemed insurmountable.

Chapter 4:
OUR EXPERIENCES WITH 'SOLUTION PROVIDERS'

As all medical solutions seemed to have failed us at this point, my family never stopped their desperate search for answers. Refusing to give up on God, we began visiting various prayer houses in hopes of divine healing. I lost count of how many prayer houses we visited—there were so many. Recommendations came from all quarters regarding places where we might find a solution. Each time my mother heard of a new place, she would drop whatever she was doing to take me there, regardless of the distance. We fasted frequently. Throughout these ventures, I received numerous revelations about the cause of the problem and potential solutions. I was given many spiritual assignments, most of which I carried out in the hope of regaining my sight. For instance, at one church, we were told that I had to live there for six months. Even though I wanted to resist, my mother tearfully pleaded with me to comply. She left everything she was doing to stay with me at the church for most of those six months.

A Fake Pastor scammed us

At another church, the pastor demanded a substantial sum of money, promising to restore my sight within two weeks. Hearing this, my parents scrambled to borrow the money, as they had none. After securing the money and giving it to the pastor, he provided me with a liquid in a small bottle, instructing me to apply it morning and night. When the two weeks passed without any miracle, we returned to the pastor, who began blaming me. He accused me of faithlessness, claiming that my lack of faith was the reason the treatment didn't work. In anguish, I wondered what more I could have done. Was visiting his church not enough faith? Was borrowing money we didn't have not enough faith? Was applying the liquid not enough faith? We later discovered that the pastor was a scammer.

While many of these experiences helped build my faith, they also exposed numerous corrupt practices being perpetrated by some clergy and so-called spiritual leaders. These revelations changed my perspective for many years.

Felix: Brother By blood, Friend by Choice

"The ordeal we went through as a family could only be likened to the Great Disappointment of 1844 when William Miller's failed prophecy left countless souls shattered. In our own lives, we faced a similar moment of profound disappointment, one that tested the very fabric of our family's faith, love, and resilience.

Our family was built on love—the kind of love that made us ready to sacrifice anything for one another. Yet, as Chidi's vision faded at an alarming rate, this love was put to the ultimate test. The diagnosis of glaucoma came like a dark cloud over our lives, but nothing could prepare us for how rapidly the disease would rob Chidi of his sight. It was as if the world grew dimmer with each passing day.

The doctors diagnosed glaucoma, A thief of sight, they said, that could be managed with continuous treatment to reduce ocular pressure. But the truth was more grim than their prognosis. The disease advanced like a storm, ravaging Chidi's vision far faster than anyone had expected. We believed in God, of course, but as the darkness closed in, we realized that our faith needed to deepen. We needed answers—desperately, urgently—and we were willing to listen to anything that seemed like the voice of God.

A Family's Faith Tested

We came from a long line of Seventh-day Adventists, a family deeply rooted in tradition, where our ways of life and beliefs were as conservative as they were unwavering. Anything that strayed from the path of simple prayer and pure faith was seen as spiritism, a compromise that we dared not entertain. Yet, here we were, faced with the unimaginable. At that moment, I knew I was willing to break every rule, cross every line, and do whatever it took—beyond our religious beliefs—to save Chidi from a life of darkness.

When we were directed to a spiritualist, it felt as though we were stepping onto forbidden ground. This man, with his strange rituals and mysterious air, offered a solution that sent shivers down our spines. Chidi, he said, must bathe in a river at night for seven consecutive days. Each night, a new sponge would be used, and at the end of the bath, it would be thrown into the flowing water. The river, with its currents and whispers, would carry away all the evil and sickness, or so he claimed. Prayers and chants would accompany the ritual, invoking forces we barely understood.

This was no small task. It was a test, not just of faith, but of courage, as it went against everything we had been taught. Papa, staunch in his beliefs, objected vehemently. He wanted nothing to do with it and distanced himself entirely. But I, driven by desperation and a fierce determination to save my brother, took on the responsibility. I would do anything—anything that could bring a solution to this terrifying problem.

The Journey to the River

The biggest hurdle wasn't just the ritual itself, but finding a suitable river for the exercise. The nearest river, one we could access without arousing suspicion, was close to my maternal home. Chidi and I concocted a plan, requesting a visit to our maternal relatives under the guise of spending time with them.

Our parents, oblivious to our true intentions, agreed. Once we arrived, we confided in our maternal uncle, explaining our desperate situation and asking for his help. A loving and compassionate man, he couldn't refuse us. He agreed to let us stay and even offered to support us in whatever way he could.

The first night felt like the beginning of an epic journey, one filled with dread and uncertainty. We were accompanied by one of our cousins, a boy much younger than Chidi, but brave beyond his years. As we approached the river, the darkness seemed to grow thicker, more oppressive. The path was overgrown, the air thick with the scent of wet earth and decaying leaves. The river itself was a wild, untamed thing, its waters dark and mysterious. The cries of unseen animals echoed in the distance, and the songs of birds—some melodious, others terrifying—added to the eerie atmosphere.

The spot we chose was littered with debris, decayed leaves, and floating plants. We used long sticks to clear the surface, our hands trembling with fear. What could be lurking beneath those murky waters? The thought sent chills down our spines, but hope—foolish, desperate hope—overrode our fears. We sang songs, our voices quivering, and prayed as if our lives depended on it. I helped Chidi undress, his body shivering not just from the cold but from the fear that clung to us both. The bath was solemn, almost sacred, but instead of a sense of peace, we felt only the weight of despair. The river moved with a slow, deliberate current, carrying our tears away into the night. When it was over, I helped him out, his steps unsteady, and we made our way back, silent and heavy-hearted.

Each evening, as the sun dipped below the horizon, a familiar dread took hold. The sights of that place—the dark, foreboding river—were enough to make our hearts race with fear. The second night, our younger cousin, who had accompanied us the first time, refused to go. His fear was too great. He was much younger than us, so we couldn't blame him. So, Chidi and I went alone, our faith stronger than our fear. We believed—no, we knew—that heaven would hear our cries, that

God would reach down and touch the earth in response to our prayers.

By the fifth night, the terror of the river had dulled slightly, replaced by a resigned determination. The sounds that had once filled us with fear became familiar, almost comforting in their predictability. We wished we could rush through the week, fold it up like an old, unwanted napkin, and put it behind us. But time moved slowly, each day longer than the last.

The Final Night and Aftermath

The final night arrived—a Saturday. We approached the ritual with a mix of faith and exhaustion. We performed the bath one last time, our hearts heavy with the weight of expectation. But when it was over, nothing had changed. We emerged from the river, our hope shattered, and we cried—cried as we had never cried before. Did God hear us? Did He see our sacrifice, our desperate pleas? In that moment, we could have lost faith, but instead, something miraculous happened. In our brokenness, His love and grace began to heal us, piece by piece.

Victims of Deception

Our desperation led us down darker paths. We fell into the hands of other spiritualists, charlatans who preyed on our vulnerability. One such man, with a wicked gleam in his eye, claimed that Chidi's problem stemmed from satanic nails embedded in his body, preventing the medication from working. Each nail, he said, had to be removed—at a price, of course. His method was grotesque. He would press his mouth to Chidi's skin, draw in a deep breath, and then spit out nails into a bowl. The pain was real, the blood was real, but the nails? They were *nothing but a cruel trick. We paid for hundreds of nails, believing each time that we were one step closer to healing, until we could no longer afford his wickedness.*

Seeking God beyond Healing

In the end, our journey led us to a profound realization: we had to stop seeking God merely for the miracle we longed for and start seeking Him for who He truly is. The weight of our suffering and desperation had driven us to an intense focus on our need for physical healing. Yet, amid the tears and the relentless darkness, we began to understand a deeper truth.

We shifted our gaze from the fleeting hope of a miracle to the eternal and unchanging essence of God's presence. We sought not just for a solution to our immediate pain but for an intimate encounter with His divine love and guidance. It was in this shift that we discovered a treasure far more valuable than physical healing—a treasure of spiritual depth and richness that could only be found in the heart of God.

Now blind, Chidi was led by God in ways beyond our understanding. The blindness that had once seemed like an insurmountable obstacle became a canvas for God's extraordinary work. Through his sightlessness, Chidi experienced divine guidance and clarity in ways that transcended the physical realm. God's presence became a beacon, illuminating paths and possibilities that Chidi could never have navigated on his own. It was as if the blindness had stripped away the distractions, allowing him to see more clearly with his spirit than he ever could with his eyes.

For me, the journey through darkness and pain was transformative. It was not just a trial but a deepening of my faith. The process of surrendering our demands for physical healing allowed me to discover a faith that was more profound and resilient than anything I had previously known. I came to understand that God's presence could fill the void left by our unmet desires, and His love could be a source of strength and peace amidst our struggles. It was through this transformation that I found a deeper connection with God, one that was rooted in His character rather than in our circumstances.

To all who read this, I urge you to seek God not merely for the miracles you desire but for who He is. His power extends far beyond the physical realm, reaching into the depths of our hearts and souls. It's not only about the answers to our prayers but about the journey of encountering His divine presence. God's guidance lights our path through the darkest valleys, and His brilliance shines in ways that never fade. Embrace the fullness of His love and presence, for it is in this divine relationship that we find the true essence of healing and hope.

'Felix'

Mr. Ubong and his Medicine

In our relentless search for a solution, we visited a place that wasn't a church but rather a local doctor who used roots and herbs for treatment. This experience is one I will never forget. A recommendation led us to this practitioner, located in a distant state. When we arrived with my parents and two older brothers, the doctor informed us that the medicine he would use required me to stay with him. He said that for the treatment to be effective, I needed to live with him for at least five months.

By this time, my four older siblings were scattered in different states due to their jobs and studies. My immediate older brother, Felix, was in college, while my sister Blessing, our youngest sibling, was in high school. To complicate matters, my father was very ill. The village was one of the most remote places I had ever seen, with no electricity, no internet, and a significant language barrier—I couldn't understand their language, and they couldn't understand mine. Since most people there neither spoke nor understood English, communication was even more difficult.

After considering these harsh realities, including the distance and the difficulties, my family decided I should not stay there. No one could stay with me since my mother needed to care for my sick and aging father, and my siblings were tied up with their own commitments.

That night, back at home, I couldn't sleep. My mind was flooded with thoughts. I thought about the school I was missing, the pain I felt each morning when I heard my peers passing by our house on their way to school, and each afternoon when they returned. I thought about my mother's daily tears, which were killing me slowly, and the pitying looks from visitors who came to our house, making me feel as if I were already dead. After hours of agonizing contemplation, I concluded that I must go to that village, even if it meant staying there alone.

I wanted to be far from everyone and believed that trying something, whether it worked or not, was better than not trying at all. Although I was highly pessimistic, I felt that in my desperate situation, I had to hold on to some hope and keep trying.

The hardest part was telling my mother about my decision to live alone in such a distant and unfamiliar place, given my condition. I knew this decision would deeply traumatize both her and my already sick father, so I was afraid to break the news. But I knew I had to be honest, which I did with great courage. Upon hearing this, they were devastated and pleaded with me to reconsider.

Despite their pleas, I remained resolute. They began calling my siblings, asking them to talk me out of my plan. My siblings also tried to persuade me to change my mind, but I couldn't. I told them that staying at home and potentially falling into depression—possibly leading to death—was a worse option than going. With fear, they reluctantly allowed me to go. I still remember the sorrowful tears my parents shed as I prepared for this difficult journey.

With the limited funds available, my mother managed to buy some essentials and a small mattress for me. On the departure day, my parents and my immediate older brother, who had returned from school to accompany me, set off for the unfamiliar land where I would isolate myself.

The Journey Begins

Getting to Uron, Mr. Ubong and his family warmly welcomed us and encouraged me to have faith that their medicine would be effective. The man explained how much he would charge for the treatment and the deposit required before starting. With the little money my siblings contributed, we were able to make the deposit. It was agreed that they would feed me, and we would pay them at the end of the month, which we readily consented to. After finalizing the agreement, my family needed to leave due to the long journey back home. As they were about to depart, I felt as though I had been left in a lonely abyss of despair. It was as if a floodgate of tears was opened. We all began to cry, hugging each other as if we were not going to see each other again. My mother tried to convince me to come back with them, as she couldn't bear the thought of leaving me behind in that obscure village. But I told her it was too late. The sorrow in the room was so intense that even Mr. Ubong's family joined in the tears. When my family finally left, it felt as though I was all alone in a vast, lonely, and dark world.

As I was led to the room that would be my new home, I quickly realized I had signed up for an adventure I never bargained for. "Challenging" didn't even begin to describe it. The room was small—so small that if I stretched too enthusiastically, I might accidentally high-five both walls at once. There was no ceiling, no plastered walls, and no tiled floor—just the bare, rough earth beneath my feet, whispering, *Welcome to survival mode, my friend.*

The only piece of furniture was a modest bed that looked like it had lived through several generations of hardship. Luxury? That word had long since packed its bags and left this place. My one source of comfort? The tiny radio my uncle had given me for the journey. It became my companion, my therapist, and my escape from the reality I had voluntarily walked into.

Now, let's talk about the bathroom situation—or rather, the complete lack of one. The toilet was a pit latrine sitting far in the backyard, as though exiled for crimes unknown. Two parallel logs of wood stretched over the pit, and that was where one was expected to perch like a circus act in perfect balance. Falling was not an option. I made a silent vow to develop core strength at all costs.

The "bathroom" was equally remarkable—an open-air masterpiece crafted from rusty corrugated iron sheets that had seen better days. No roof, no privacy, just nature's full embrace. When it rained, you had two choices: either embrace the impromptu shower or flee, soapy and confused, into the nearest shelter. I had a feeling I'd be doing both soon enough.

As if these trials weren't enough, I faced another daunting hurdle: language. The villagers spoke in rapid, animated bursts of their local dialect, and believe me, I loved every sound of it, but I... well, didn't understand it; I spoke English, which wasn't much use in this part of the world.

That first night, regret hit me like a ton of bricks. *Why had I come? What was I thinking?* I stared at the food they set before me, my appetite vanishing faster than my enthusiasm. It wasn't that the food was bad—far from it. This part of Nigeria boasted some of the most delicious dishes I had ever known. But my heart was too heavy to eat. I curled up on my bed, tears slipping down my face. I wanted to go home. I wanted my family. I wanted comfort.

But the next morning, something remarkable happened. After whispering a desperate prayer, I felt a deep, calming reassurance settle over me. It was as if God Himself had leaned in and whispered, *You're going to be okay.* And somehow, I believed it.

With renewed determination, I decided I had two choices: drown in my misery or learn to swim in this unfamiliar sea. I chose the latter. First, I needed to communicate. I found an unlikely ally in the man's last wife, a kind woman who understood a bit of English. With her help, I quickly mastered the crucial phrases: how to ask for food, request help, and—most importantly—where to find the toilet before disaster struck. It turns out necessity really *is* the mother of invention.

Armed with my new language skills, I ventured into the world of socializing. The man's children were initially amused by my struggle, but once I could string together a few words, they warmed up to me. Life became a little easier.

But let's not forget the pit latrine—a horror that no amount of language skills could ease. The stench was legendary, the kind that punched you in the face before you even got close. Flies buzzed around like they were throwing a victory party, and I had no choice but to crash it. Each trip to that latrine was a mental and physical challenge, requiring deep breaths and strong resolve.

The bathroom situation remained an ongoing battle. Bathing under the open sky meant always being at the mercy of the elements. If a rainstorm decided to make an appearance mid-bath, you had no choice but to let nature take its course. At this point, modesty was a luxury I couldn't afford.

With no phone, no internet, and no one to talk to, my small radio became my lifeline. It was my friend, my storyteller, and my only connection to the outside world. Every night, I clung to it, listening to distant voices that reminded me I wasn't alone.

Through it all, I learned something invaluable—humans are incredibly adaptable. When stripped of comfort, we find strength we never knew we had. We survive. We endure. And sometimes, we even laugh at the absurdity of it all.

And so, in that tiny, ceiling-less room, with my pit latrine nightmares and rain-soaked showers, I discovered something life-changing: if you can't change your circumstances, change your attitude.

Because sometimes, all you really need to survive is a little faith, a little humor, and a whole lot of mosquito repellent.

The Cost of Hope: Fire in my Eyes

If pain had a face, I was certain it looked like that eye medicine Mr. Ubong administered with such unwavering dedication. The moment the fiery concoction touched my eyes; it felt like someone had summoned all the demons of hell and assigned them the singular task of setting my eyeballs ablaze. Mornings and nights became battlegrounds where I braced myself for war, my only weapon being the sheer hope that I wouldn't pass out from the agony. The searing pain scrambled my thoughts, leaving me in a delirious haze, questioning every life choice that had led me to this moment.

Just when I thought my days would be an endless loop of torment, fate decided to cut me some slack. Mr. Ubong's son, a college student, came home for the holidays, and suddenly, I had a lifeline. Not only did he take a liking to me, but he also became my escape from the dreary routine of suffering. Every evening, we'd stroll together, and for those few golden hours, I was no longer the boy enduring hellfire treatments—I was just a regular guy enjoying the simple pleasure of companionship.

His presence was like a light switch in my otherwise dim reality. But, as with all good things, the holiday came to an end, and he packed his bags, returning to school, leaving me behind like a forgotten bookmark in a half-read novel. It was as if someone had thrown me back into a well of silence.

But here's the thing about adversity—it forces you to grow in ways you never expected. By then, I had picked up enough of their language to communicate, and just like that, the once-alien environment wasn't so isolating anymore. It wasn't easy, but I learned an invaluable lesson: sometimes, survival isn't about avoiding the pain but finding the moments of relief in between.

Dwindling Hope

After a few weeks, my mother visited, and we were very excited to see each other again. She spent a few weeks with me before leaving to be with my father, who needed her support. My siblings visited from time to time, staying with me as long as they could. The way Mr. Ubong and his family touted his medicines, coupled with his assurances of my healing, made me optimistic again despite the hot and painful application. I hoped that within three months, I would see some improvement in my eyes. But one month passed then the second, and then the third—yet there was no improvement. Instead, the little sight I had was fast vanishing. At this point, I began to despair again and approached the man, expressing my worries. I told him I had been there for over three months with nothing to show for it, and that my sight was rapidly fading. He assured me again and said he would start using more sophisticated and effective medicines. However, he told me I needed to call my parents to bring more money, as these medicines were very expensive.

Another Attempt at a Cure

The last time my mother visited, I confided in her about this latest development—the need for more money to continue my treatment. Not long after she left, she returned with my father and three of my siblings. To my greatest relief, they brought the money. We spent a long and heartfelt time together, and before they departed, they handed the money to Mr. Ubong, who reassured them with confidence that this new set of medicines would restore my sight in no time.

But after they left, a deep sadness settled over me. Almost all my family's resources were being funneled into my treatment, yet there was still no sign of improvement. Guilt gnawed at me, an unshakable weight pressing on my chest.

Two days later, Mr. Ubong began administering the new medicines. Weeks passed. Then months. More than two months in, and still—nothing. No flicker of light. No sign of progress. By then, I knew in my heart that this wasn't going to work. Even Mr. Ubong, who once spoke with certainty, now seemed weary. The enthusiasm in his voice had dulled, and I could see the unspoken truth in his demeanor—he was losing faith in the process too.

By the time six months had crawled by with nothing to show for it, the thought of leaving gnawed at my mind. But leave to where? To do what? Each day, I wrestled with these unanswered questions, and with every passing moment, my despair only deepened.

Then, just when I thought I was trapped in an endless cycle of uncertainty, something utterly unexpected happened— an unforeseen twist that abruptly changed everything and sent me hurtling away from that obscure village.

Mr. Ndah, the 'Spirit-Stricken Impotent' Man

One cool evening, a motorcyclist brought two middle-aged men to Mr. Ubong's compound. Their faces were shadowed by the dim light of the setting sun. After a lengthy discussion with my host outside, they entered with an air of quiet seriousness and took their seats. Before I could grasp the situation, Mr. Ubongs's second wife was already in my room, frantically cleaning and rearranging things. I sat up, intrigued. *Why the sudden need for spring cleaning?* My living conditions had been nothing short of spartan since I arrived—why the sudden need to impress?

After the two men stepped outside, I turned to her with a raised brow. "Madam, what's with all the preparations?"

She hesitated, glancing toward the door as if to make sure no one was listening. Then, in a hushed tone laced with apprehension, she revealed, "The men will be staying with us for some time". A wave of relief washed over me. *Finally!* After enduring what felt like a lifetime of isolation, I would have new faces, fresh conversations, something—anything—to break the monotony. It felt like a prisoner suddenly discovering a cellmate.

Within a couple of days, we had started getting along quite well. In fact, Mr. Ndah and I became quite close, sharing our stories and struggles as if we were old friends.

One afternoon, I was alone in the room with Mr. Ndah—the older of the two men—and I sensed a heaviness in his demeanor as we shared the challenges that had brought us to this place. His voice was calm yet weighed down by sorrow.

Without hesitation, Mr. Ndah began to narrate his ordeal to me. His voice, calm as the sea on a moonless night, tinged with pain and regret, said, "I'm a father of four grown-up children, and the young man you see with me is my friend who brought me here." He paused for a few seconds, the room echoing with silence. Curious about the story he was about to tell, I reached out my hand toward him. "Mr. Ndah," I called out softly.

He continued, his grip tightening slightly as he held my hand—my only window to his world. "I'm a very successful man," he admitted, his tone carrying the weight of a truth he had long avoided. "I have numerous properties, hotels—wealth beyond what most can dream of."

I listened intently, but something in his voice told me this wasn't a boast. It was the prelude to a confession.

"But..." He let out another sigh, the kind that people release when they're about to confront the demons of their past. "My success blinded me. I lived recklessly, indulging in pleasures without a second thought. I was a man who never said no—to women, to desires, to anything my heart craved."

The words hung in the air, sharp and raw.

"And now," he added, almost in a whisper, "it has come back to haunt me."

At that moment, I realized that regret is a debt that life never forgets to collect. Here was a man who had everything yet carried an emptiness that wealth could never fill.

One day, in the midst of his high-flying, pleasure-seeking lifestyle, Mr. Ndah met a stunning young lady. She was the kind of woman who turned heads effortlessly—the type who could make a man forget his name, let alone his common sense. Their relationship, though fleeting, was filled with indulgence, and one night, passion led them to bed.

As he lay there afterward, basking in the warmth of self-satisfaction, the young lady turned to him with an eerie calmness and said, *"You will never be able to sleep with any other woman except me."*

He chuckled, thinking she was just being dramatic—perhaps trying to stake her claim on him, the way possessive lovers do. He had heard women say all sorts of things in the heat of emotion, but this? This was new.

"You don't mean that," he had replied, grinning, thinking she was joking.

She didn't grin back.

A few days later, reality struck.

He tried to be intimate with his wife, confident that his usual prowess would carry the night. But his manhood, which had always been as responsive as an eager student, suddenly refused to cooperate. No matter what they tried, it was as lifeless as a deflated balloon.

At first, he brushed it off as exhaustion, stress—anything but what that woman had said. But then, it happened again. And again. Days turned into weeks, and no matter what he did, no matter how hard he tried (pun painfully intended), nothing worked.

His wife, who was no stranger to his promiscuity, quickly put two and two together—and, in her anger, she made sure he felt every ounce of the consequences.

"So, you've finally met your match, eh? After all these years of running after women like a dog chasing scraps, look where it's gotten you!" she spat, her words as sharp as a whip.

The house, once a home, became a battlefield. She hurled accusations like spears, each one hitting its mark. *"You've brought shame upon this family! Do you think I don't know what you've been up to? Now look at you—cursed by your own foolishness!"*

The weight of his choices came crashing down. His pride, once built on conquest and excess, was now reduced to the wreckage of humiliation. Desperate, he set out on a quest to reclaim what he had lost—not just his dignity but the very essence of his manhood.

One doctor after another, one traditional healer after the next, one religious leader to the next. Each place promised hope; each place left him with nothing but disappointment.

This—*this*—was the fourth stop on his pilgrimage for redemption.

As he spoke, his voice wavered with a pain that no amount of wealth could erase. His eyes, dimmed by regret, searched mine as if hoping I held an answer he had yet to find.

I sat there, absorbing the weight of his confession, feeling a mix of sympathy and irony. Life, it seemed, had a cruel way of teaching lessons.

I took a deep breath and chose my words carefully. *"Mr. Ndah, life has a way of forcing us to confront the things we refuse to acknowledge. Some lessons come with whispers; others... with a hammer."*

He exhaled sharply and nodded.

I pondered his story—the bitter irony of it all. Life has a strange sense of humor. It lets us chase what we think we want, only to reveal, often too late, that we've been running in the wrong direction all along.

And so, as Mr. Ndah sat there—a man draped in wealth yet stripped of peace—I realized his story wasn't just his own; it was a lesson. *Success without wisdom is like a mansion built on sand—impressive for a while, but destined to crumble.*

"You chased pleasure, but it led you here. Maybe this isn't a curse, but a wake-up call."

He looked at me, searching for something—hope, perhaps.

"A man can own the world, but if he loses himself, what good is it?" I added, my voice gentle but firm.

Silence stretched between us—not empty, but full of reflection.

There are some stories you hear, and they entertain. Others, they haunt you. But some—like this one—they change you.

And I knew, from the way he stared off into the distance, that Mr. Ndah would never be the same again.

The Solution and the Night of Reckoning

Throughout our stay, I didn't know what solution our host was planning for Mr. Ndah's problem. However, one afternoon, the senior wife returned from the market with a fowl and other mysterious items. The clucking of the fowl was the only clue to the nature of their preparations.

That day, everyone seemed to be preparing for something, but what it was, I didn't know. Our host was engaged in a whispering conversation with Mr. Ndah and his friend at the back of the house.

Later that evening, I observed the arrival of a very old man and woman. I couldn't tell if they were husband and wife, but all of them were having a meeting so secretive that no one could hear what they were saying.

Throughout that evening, I felt uncomfortable, especially with the presence of those two old folks. Their visit, movements, and secretive discussions were highly suspicious.

Around 11 P.M., an unsettling silence fell over the house. The once lively murmurs had vanished, swallowed by the darkness. I strained my ears, hoping to catch even the faintest whisper of my companions, but there was nothing—just the eerie, empty hush that makes the skin crawl.

A gnawing unease settled in my stomach. *Where were they? What had happened?*

I sat up, my mind cycling through a thousand grim possibilities. But the more I thought about it, the heavier my eyelids became, and eventually, exhaustion dragged me into sleep.

I had barely drifted off when—BANG!

The door burst open so violently that I nearly leaped out of my skin. My heart pounded in my throat as I bolted upright, only to find Mr. Ndah standing there, his face as pale as a ghost, gasping for breath, eyes wide with terror.

"What happened? Where's your friend?" I asked, my voice barely steady.

And then, he told me.

Apparently, our host—our *beloved, trusted* host—had planned to take him to the river at midnight for a cleansing ritual. You see, Mr. Ndah had been battling a problem he hadn't exactly advertised—impotence. And according to this so-called solution, he was to bathe in the river under the watchful gaze of the night, with a fowl and a host of other ritual items meant to "appease" the spirits causing his predicament. The elderly visitors we had seen earlier? They were the officiating priests of this eerie, supernatural arrangement.

Now, *that* alone was bad enough. But fate, in its mischievous wisdom, had other plans.

As they made their way through a narrow, bushy path toward the river, a group of local youths—who had apparently caught wind of this little midnight adventure—lay in wait.

And then, they pounced.

The attackers ransacked their belongings, beat them without mercy, and sent them fleeing for their lives. Mr. Ndah, by some stroke of luck, managed to escape and run back home. But his friend, Mr. Ubong? Not so much.

"And what about Mr. Ubong?" I asked, my voice barely above a whisper.

Mr. Ndah swallowed hard, his face drenched in fear. *"Ah, my brother... he's still there,"* he stammered. *"They hit him—right where he recently had surgery, beside his stomach. He collapsed. He couldn't walk. They left him there."*

I felt the blood drain from my face.

Before I could react, wails erupted from Mr. Ubong's family. Panic spread like wildfire. The sheer horror of it all—being left helpless in the dark, wounded, in unfamiliar terrain—sent shivers down my spine.

Then, as if the night hadn't been eventful enough, the same youths stormed back into the compound, this time dragging a barely conscious Mr. Ubong on a motorcycle. His body was limp, his face contorted in agony.

His crime? Attempting a forbidden ritual at the river.

The youths, enraged, declared that sacrifices at the river were strictly prohibited. According to them, such rituals often led to mysterious drownings, and they had sworn to put an end to them. But what made them *truly* furious was the fact that Mr. Ubong—an *elder* in the community—was the one leading the charge.

Their verdict? Both Mr. Ndah and Mr. Ubong were to be taken away immediately.

A death sentence.

The air grew thick with tension. Mr. Ubong's family pleaded—begged—for mercy. They cried, they negotiated, they clung to the youths' feet, swearing by every ancestor in their lineage that such a thing would never happen again.

Finally, after what felt like an eternity, the youths relented—for now. But they left a chilling warning: *They would return at dawn to punish their kinsman.*

That night, none of us slept. Every sound made us jump. Every shadow felt like a threat. The weight of uncertainty pressed heavily on our chests.

Morning came, and with it, the inevitable.

The youths returned, this time with demands. If Mr. Ubong wanted to keep his life, he had to provide four fowls, several bottles of dry gin, kola nuts, and a substantial amount of money.

Desperate to buy peace, he agreed. But then, he had a clever idea.

"Help us find the missing man," he proposed.

Surprisingly, the youths agreed. Perhaps guilt gnawed at them, or maybe they simply enjoyed the thrill of the hunt. Either way, they set out into the thick forest, scouring every bush, every clearing, calling out for him.

By 10 A.M., they found him.

There, under a tree, deep in the wilderness, he lay—fast asleep.

Yes. Asleep.

This man had gone through a brutal beating, fled for his life, and in the middle of nowhere, decided, *You know what? This seems like a good spot for a nap.*

They shook him awake, half-amused, half-annoyed, and dragged him back home.

The moment he returned, Mr. Ndah and his friend wasted no time. They threw their belongings into their bags with the speed of men who had seen the gates of hell swing open and had no intention of sticking around.

And just like that, they were gone.

As the dust settled, a heavy silence fell upon the house. The only sound was Mr. Ubong's deep groans, his body wrecked with pain from the night's ordeal.

And then, it hit me.

Mr. Ubong wasn't just an *herbalist*. He wasn't just some kind old man with a love for roots and leaves.

He was a *dibia*—a ritualist.

He had fooled us all. Fooled my parents. Fooled *me*. Had I known, I would never have set foot in his house. My family would have never allowed it.

Frustration churned within me.

I had come here in search of healing, and now, my supposed "healer" lay bedridden, while my own condition remained untouched, ignored.

Was this all a joke? A colossal waste of time?

I thought about leaving. About running as far from this madness as I could. But there was one problem—I had no way to contact my family. No phone. No letters. No one to come and get me. And so, I remained

Days passed.

Loneliness settled into my bones, wrapping around me like a cold, unwelcome embrace.

And all I could do was wait.

A Miraculous Arrival

As dawn broke, painting the sky with strokes of gold and crimson, the village slowly stirred awake, revealing its mix of joy and sorrow, triumph and trial. But on this particular morning, fate had something extraordinary in store for me.

I woke up later than usual, the weight of past days still pressing on my body like a heavy cloak. Then—tap, tap, tap—a soft, measured knock sounded against the rickety wooden door of my dimly lit room.

For a moment, I hesitated. I assumed it was one of Mr. Ubong's wives or children, perhaps bringing food or calling me to some mundane village task. But as I pulled the creaky door open, what I saw nearly stopped my heart.

My mother, there she stood—my sweet, beautiful mother—her presence as radiant as the first rays of morning sunlight breaking through the bleakest winter night. A rush of emotions surged through me—relief, joy, disbelief, gratitude—so strong they nearly brought me to my knees.

"Mama!" The word escaped my lips in a breathless whisper before I threw myself into her waiting arms.

I held onto her tightly, as if letting go would make her vanish. For months, I had endured loneliness, fear, and despair, trapped in a place that had become my crucible of pain. And now, she was here—my rescuer, my anchor, my beacon of hope.

She held me just as tightly, her embrace full of love, full of promise, full of home. Though her face was lined with exhaustion from the grueling journey, her spirit remained unshaken. Her hands, worn but strong, gently cupped my face as she whispered, *"It's over, my son. I'm taking you home."*

Tears welled in my eyes. How could I ever put into words the depth of my gratitude?

Despite the fatigue gnawing at her bones, my mother wasted no time. She had come prepared, armed with enough funds to settle the remaining balance for the treatment and to arrange for our swift departure from this place that had held me captive in uncertainty for far too long.

As we packed my meager belongings, I felt a flood of emotions—relief so immense it nearly left me breathless, gratitude so profound it filled **every** inch of my soul. The weight that had pressed on my heart for months was finally lifting, giving way to a sense of freedom I had almost forgotten.

When we finally stepped out of the house, ready to leave, I turned to glance at the village one last time. A strange mix of sadness and liberation washed over me. This place had been a battleground—a test of endurance, faith, and resilience. It had brought me pain, yet it had also refined me, like gold in fire.

As our journey home began, the winding roads stretched endlessly before us, but I hardly noticed. My heart was too full. Every bump, every turn was a reminder that I was inching closer to the place where I truly belonged.

Through the rhythmic hum of the vehicle, I sat in deep reflection, staring out at the vast, open landscape. I had lost so much, yet I had gained something even greater—the unshakable realization of my own strength, the unwavering support of my family, and the undeniable truth that hope is never truly lost.

And then, finally, home.

The moment we arrived, my family rushed toward me, arms wide, voices choked with emotion. They held me close as if to reassure themselves that I was really there, safe and whole. Their relief was palpable, their joy mirroring my own.

Even though my sight had not been restored, and the treatment had failed to deliver the miracle we had hoped for, I felt anything but defeated.

Because I had won something even greater.

I had conquered despair. I had tasted the depth of my own endurance. I had seen, in its purest form, the power of love—the kind that spans distances, withstands trials, and never wavers, no matter the storm.

This journey—though riddled with hardship—had reshaped me. It had tested my faith, my resolve, my very spirit, and through it all, I had emerged stronger, wiser, and filled with a renewed determination to keep fighting, to keep believing, to keep moving forward.

Because as long as I had faith, as long as I had family, I knew I would always find my way.

Chapter 5:
COMING TO TERMS WITH BLINDNESS

Four years had passed since I left school. Four years wasted, achieving nothing. But the most depressing part wasn't just the lost time—it was the uncertainty. I had no idea what to do next or what the future held. Since the onset of my visual impairment, everyone's efforts had been geared towards the recovery of my sight. No one had thought beyond that. Consequently, all my consciousness had been centered on the miracle of sight restoration. I never quite believed one could still live a normal life and achieve their dreams while blind. I think this was largely because I had never seen anyone my age in such a condition.

As all my consciousness revolved around sight recovery and all our efforts were channeled towards that, it became painfully clear that I might not be able to see again. I was left with deep clouds of anxiety and depression hanging in my mental sky. The prospect of going back to school now seemed beyond the realm of possibility. By day, I was hounded by a corroding sense of emptiness, and by night, haunted by a depressing sense of nothingness. My outlook on the future became grim and bleak. At this point in my life, I was almost tempted to cry out with Shakespeare's Macbeth, "Life is a tale told by an idiot, full of sound and fury, signifying nothing."

The Role of My Faith

Having relied for so long on human effort and seeing how this effort had crashed at my feet, hope became forlorn. With little or no strength left to build courage again, I knew for sure that at this phase of my life's tough journey, only divine assistance could sustain me and carry me through. With this dazzling new consciousness that was born in me, I realized that a new light was rising upon me, and I could not hesitate to follow its guidance. Hence, rather than keep despairing and possibly fall into self-destructive habits, I encouraged myself in the Lord. Heeding our Master's call, "Come to me, all who labor and are heavily laden," I went to Jesus with the heavy yoke of blindness and surrendered all to Him in prayer. Once again, I withdrew— not to myself this time, but to God, my Father and Creator, who knows the thoughts He has towards me, thoughts not of evil but of good, to give me a future and a hope. I gave myself to fasting and prayer. Every day, I fasted and prayed as if my life depended on it.

Now, I was no longer asking God for sight, but to know His purpose for my life. I also prayed for comfort and strength to carry on living out His purpose for my life, even if it meant I would never see again with my two eyes. Amazingly, the more I pressed deeper into this abiding faith in God, the more I was strengthened, comforted, and encouraged. There is no doubt that the Lord heard me from His high heaven as I daily sought Him and cried out to Him.

Gratitude: My Lifeline

During my intimate moments with God through prayer, I found that one of the most profound ways He helped me come to terms with blindness was by planting within me a deep and abiding sense of gratitude. At first, it was difficult to see beyond the pain and uncertainty of my condition, but gratitude became the lens through which I began to perceive life anew.

As I prayed and reflected, my mind traveled back to those perilous moments during my ordeal—times when I could have stumbled into a water-filled pit, walked unknowingly into the path of an oncoming truck, or perished in some other tragic way.

Yet, in every instance, an unseen hand had preserved me. I began to understand that my survival was not a matter of luck or chance, but of divine providence.

Then, I thought of those whose voices had been permanently silenced by death—those who could no longer utter a prayer, whose stories had ended before they had the chance to rewrite them. I considered those who, though alive, had lost their minds to insanity and were unable to form coherent thoughts, much less commune with God. Others lay in deep comas, trapped in unconsciousness, unable to utter a single word of supplication. And yet, here I was—blind, but alive. Struggling, but still standing. Hurting, but still capable of hope.

One memory struck me with particular intensity. At the early stage of my eye condition, there was a young friend of mine—my age mate and my look-alike. Whenever my mother saw him, she would break down in tears because he reminded her so much of me and the painful reality of my condition. And yet, in a cruel twist of fate, this young man—full of life, with seemingly endless possibilities ahead of him—died in a motor accident. The weight of this realization pressed upon me. Why was I still here? Why had I been spared while others had perished?

In the quiet of my heart, an answer emerged—not in a thunderous voice, but in a gentle whisper of understanding. Life is not measured by what is taken from us, but by what remains and how we choose to use it. I could not change my blindness, but I could decide how to respond to it. I could either drown in self-pity or rise in gratitude. And so, I chose to be grateful.

Gratitude became more than an emotion; it became a force of healing. The more I gave thanks, the more I felt peace settle within me. I realized that gratitude does not deny pain; rather, it shifts the focus from loss to love, from despair to hope, from what is missing to what still remains. Each moment of thanksgiving reminded me that God, who had carried me through my darkest valleys, was not about to abandon me in the future. The past became my testimony; the present, my opportunity; and the future, a journey of trust.

This revelation reshaped my perspective. I w.
walking the lonely path of blindness alone—God was with me
every step of the way. The more I embraced this truth, the more
my fears diminished, replaced by a quiet yet unshakable
confidence. The road ahead remained uncertain, but I no longer
feared it. If I had been preserved thus far, then surely, I was
meant to keep moving forward.

And so, I walk—not in bitterness, not in regret, but in
gratitude. For in gratitude, I have found strength. In gratitude, I
have found healing. And in gratitude, I have found the courage to
face whatever lies ahead.

4o

.

Visions: Another Lifeline

During my intimate moments with God, another way He helped
me overcome the pain of blindness was through the visions He
granted me in my dreams. Often, after praying and going to bed,
I would dream of myself in more favorable conditions and
circumstances. I saw many great and promising things about my
life. Sometimes, I would see myself on a very high mountain,
standing before a vast crowd that had gathered to celebrate me.
Other times, I dreamed of leading other blind people. There was
even a time when I saw myself regaining my sight and running
around joyfully in overwhelming jubilation. On another
occasion, I saw myself walking on water, towing a ship with a
rope. These dreams were vivid and numerous, and each time I
shared them with my family, they were left in awe. It wasn't that
they didn't believe in my dreams; they simply wondered how
such things could be possible. Eventually, they started calling me
'Joseph the Dreamer.'

On one hand, I was grappling with blindness and all its
restrictive, debilitating forces. On the other hand, I was seeing a

lofty and sublime life and future in my visions. There was no doubt that my dreams stood in stark contrast to my real-life circumstances. Faced with these two opposing realities, I had two choices: to walk by the perception of my physical realities or to live by faith in my dreams. By God's grace, I chose the latter path and let my dreams guide me. The more I lived by these dreams, the more I refused to let my physical challenges deter or discourage me. Instead, I allowed these dreams to shape my perspective and outlook on life. Eventually, I stopped evaluating myself based on my environmental, hereditary, or physical challenges. Instead, I assessed my self-worth and value through the strength of those visions. I didn't just believe in those golden dreams and visions; I lived each day as if they were already reality. They transformed and influenced my mindset, thoughts, desires, aspirations, and decisions as I moved forward. Even on the meandering and frightening journey of blindness, with God's grace being sufficient, I have continued to stride forward into the future, knowing that the future rewards those who believe in their dreams.

The Word and Promises of God

Another lifeline I had was the Word of God. The Scriptures played a crucial role in helping me overcome the daunting challenge of blindness. Let me quickly say this: The Word of God is spirit, and it is alive. It has the power to accomplish what it promises; never take it for granted. "Faith comes by hearing, and hearing by the Word of God." Since I couldn't go back to school at this point, and seeing it as something almost beyond the realm of possibility, I turned to the Word of God to draw strength and inspiration. Every day, when my father was less busy, he would come and read the English Bible to me, and when my mother had time, she would read the Igbo version, which is my native language. I asked them to find passages where God speaks about light and His promises to the afflicted. Amazingly, one of the first passages they brought to me was from the book of Prophet Isaiah 42:16, where the Lord promises to lead the blind by ways they have not known, to guide them along unfamiliar paths, to turn darkness into light before them, and to make rough places smooth. As they read these glorious words to me daily, I wholeheartedly believed them, as if God were speaking directly to me and addressing my situation. Happily, I memorized these words. They became my watchwords. Believing and holding onto them each day, and every time I stepped out onto those unknown and dangerous paths, I moved and walked with audacious confidence, knowing that I did not walk alone.

At this point, I was less concerned with what the doctors had said about my condition; my confidence now rested in what God said about me. As I lived every day by the Word of God, I grew increasingly stronger, more encouraged, and more inspired. No tears or words of pity could demoralize or deter me. No blinding darkness could debilitate me any longer. I was fortified. The power of the Word of God at work in my life transformed me into a beacon of hope and strengthened my once-feeble knees.

Take This Home:

Has life's disappointments left you feeling shattered, as though your strength has drained away and giving up is the only option? Do you feel like the weight of your struggles is too much to bear, that the doors of opportunity have been slammed shut, and that hope is slipping through your fingers like sand?

Why give up? Why let despair have the final say when the One who holds the universe in His hands is still writing your story?

God is able—more than able. He is the One who breathes life into dry bones, who makes a way in the wilderness, who turns mourning into joy. Your pain is not the end of your journey; it is the birthing ground of a greater testimony. If I could find strength in my darkest moments—when I was blinded by circumstances beyond my control, when I felt lost and uncertain of what lay ahead—then so can you. Because the same God who lifted me is with you, even now.

No matter how fierce the storm, how deep the valley, or how hopeless the night may seem, know this: God has not forgotten you. He is working, even in the silence. He is weaving purpose into your pain, turning your trials into stepping stones for a greater victory.

So, rise again. Lift your eyes beyond the temporary darkness and fix them on the One who calls you His own. Hold on to faith, for even the smallest seed of belief can move mountains. Take heart—your story is far from over, and the best is yet to come.

Chapter 6:
THE LIGHT OF EDUCATION

At this stage of my journey, determined to surmount my disability, I courageously mounted up with the golden wings of faith. There was no doubt that I flew above the limiting barriers of fear and despair. Yet, I realized that without action, my flapping wings of faith wouldn't take me far. I knew that faith without works is dead. While I had relied on the unflinching love, care, and support of my family, which had elevated me to sublime heights of hope, strength, and courage, I also understood that I must one day stand on my own as a man. I trusted God for His help, but I knew that He would not allow me to achieve through prayer what I should achieve through my own effort and work. Despite my family's concern and support, I knew they would be prouder to see me rise above my disability and do something meaningful.

At this point, a new consciousness was awakening within me—a consciousness of responsibility and action. I began to recall the stories of individuals who were blind but rose above their disability to become remarkable figures in history, as the doctor had mentioned during one of our hospital visits. Each day, as I remembered these inspiring stories, I knew I had reached a pivotal point in my life where drastic action was necessary.

Rather than reacting with bitterness and despair, I began seeking ways to transform my ordeal into a creative force. Instead of surrendering to the despair and darkness of blindness, I searched for ways to turn that darkness into a creative light of success. Though this zeal burned within me, I was still uncertain about what specific action I needed to take. It was a great conundrum.

During this period of confusion, an aunt of mine, whom we hadn't seen for a long time, visited us. After learning about my predicament, she felt deeply saddened. Before leaving, she told us about a special school for the blind near where she lived.

She had once visited the school to make a donation and was amazed by how the students read, wrote, and performed other activities. When I heard this, I was shocked that blind people could still attend school. I was overwhelmed with joy; it felt as though my sight had been restored. My parents were equally thrilled. I knew instantly that the breakthrough I had prayed for had finally come. As Victor Hugo once said, "There is nothing like an idea whose time has come." I knew my time to take action had arrived. I remember that night well—I couldn't sleep, lying there on my bed, smiling, thinking, and planning how to make the most of this golden opportunity.

My father wasted no time. The next day, he traveled to the school, but unfortunately, they were already on holiday and wouldn't resume for another three weeks. When he returned with this news, I was somewhat disappointed because I couldn't wait to be enrolled. However, I found comfort in the fact that we had discovered the school and knew where it was. Among my family members, friends, and relatives, everyone who heard about this latest development was happy for me. During this period, my thoughts were consumed by the prospect of returning to school. Most of my conversations revolved around this opportunity. I could hardly stop talking about it.

Those three weeks felt like three years. I couldn't wait. While we anxiously awaited the end of the break, my mother, with money contributed by my siblings, began buying some of the things I would need for school. The feeling was like that of a child being taken to school for the first time after a long stay at home. I couldn't wait for the day to come.

Going Back to School as a Blind Man

I can't forget the day I left for school; I was the happiest man on earth. My eldest sister took two days off from her job to accompany me. As we were leaving, my parents were as happy as I was. While we were walking out of the house, I sensed my mother crying again. I was frustrated and asked her why she was doing this after seeing that I now had the opportunity to continue my education. She answered, "Chidi, my son, I am crying for joy. My tears are of joy, seeing that after all you've been through, you have finally found a new path to your future and a new purpose for your life." My mum is one of those precious souls who express their emotions through tears—they cry when angry, shed tears when happy, and sob when sad—and she has a way of making others cry with her. So, my sister and I started crying too, though this time, it wasn't out of sorrow but of joy and gratitude.

The journey to the school was fast and smooth, about an hour. When we finally arrived, I was greeted by a serene and comforting atmosphere. The whole place was so cool and quiet, and I immediately felt at home. The school was located on the outskirts of town, far from the noise and busyness that could be overwhelming for a blind person.

After completing the registration process, my sister and I were ready to go to my hostel. The hostel master asked us to wait a few minutes while he called some students to help carry my belongings. When they arrived, their voices sounded young and lively, and I asked my sister who they were. To her surprise, she realized they were students at the school. Vibrantly and gallantly, they carried my things as we followed behind. My sister, curious about whether the boys could see, was even more astonished when the hostel master revealed that they were all blind.

As we entered the hostel, I heard the voices of children around four or five years old playing and running. Initially, I thought they were the children of staff members, but when one of them bumped into me in the corridor, I realized they were blind too. I felt compassion for them being blind at such a young age, but I was also encouraged to see others younger than me facing similar challenges. The students in my hostel welcomed me warmly, and words couldn't express how glad I was to finally have the opportunity to communicate and connect with others who shared my condition. I was eager to learn about their experiences as well.

My sister, too, was encouraged to see what the other students were accomplishing despite their blindness. After she left, some of the students gathered around my bed, introduced themselves, and asked me many questions, which I excitedly answered.

Faith Becomes My Friend

Among all the students, one stood out like a bright star in a dark sky—an inquisitive boy named Faith, who would later become my best friend. As fate would have it, his bed was right next to mine, which meant I had a front-row seat to his boundless energy and endless curiosity.

The moment the other students cleared out, Faith turned to me with an eager grin. "Want a tour?" he asked, his voice full of excitement. I nodded, and just like that, he took me under his wing.

Navigating the school with Faith was like following a human GPS—except with way more personality. He knew every twist and turn, every shortcut and hidden corner, guiding me with the confidence of someone who had memorized every inch of the place. Not once did we get lost, not even when he insisted on showing me "a secret spot" that turned out to be nothing more than a quiet bench under a tree.

As we walked, I bombarded him with questions—about the school, the students, the teachers, and of course, about him. Faith answered each one with patience, humor, and a touch of mischief, as if he enjoyed watching my curiosity unfold. By the time we returned to our dorm, I already knew one thing for sure: this was the beginning of an unforgettable friendship.

My encounter with Braille

When we returned to the room, Faith handed me a book filled with raised dots and encouraged me to feel it with my fingers. I hesitated but did as he asked, running my hands over the strange patterns. My brow furrowed as confusion set in—I couldn't make sense of what I was touching.

"What is this?" I asked, my voice laced with uncertainty.

Faith smiled knowingly. "That's Braille," he said. "It's our way of reading here, and it's one of the first things you'll learn."

His words sent a wave of anxiety through me. My palms grew damp, and my breath quickened as doubt crept into my mind. How could anyone possibly read through touch? The concept felt impossibly foreign, like deciphering an alien language without a single reference point.

Faith chuckled, sensing my apprehension. "I felt the same way when I first got here," he admitted. Taking the book from my hands, he placed his fingers over the raised dots and began to read aloud. His movements were fluid and confident, as though his fingertips had eyes of their own.

I was stunned. "Wait—stop," I interrupted. "How are you doing that?"

He paused and placed my hands over his, guiding my fingers along the patterns. I tried to mimic his movements, tracing the bumps as he did, but the symbols remained an unreadable mystery to me. Frustration swelled in my chest.

Faith closed the book and patted my shoulder. "Relax," he said reassuringly. "You'll get the hang of it. It takes patience."

Determined to reassure me, he pulled out a strange plastic board that opened like a book. "This is a slate," he explained, running his fingers over its surface. "It's like a notebook, but for Braille." The slate had neat rows of small rectangular cells, each containing six tiny holes—three on one side and three on the other. "Everything we write in Braille comes from these six dots."

Then, he handed me a small metal tool with a pointed tip. "This is a stylus—it's our version of a pen." Demonstrating with practiced ease, he inserted a thick sheet of Braille paper into the slate, closed it, and began punching the dots with the stylus. Each press left an imprint, forming letters I couldn't yet understand.

If that wasn't enough to astonish me, Faith then brought out a typewriter. But this wasn't just any typewriter—it had fewer keys than the ones I had seen before. As he struck the keys, a rhythmic tapping filled the room. "This is how we type," he said, smiling. "You'll learn this too."

I was awestruck. I had spent so long feeling trapped by my blindness, never realizing there was an entire world of tools designed to empower people like me. A new thought crept into my mind—what if I had discovered this place sooner? What else had I been missing?

Before I could dwell on it, a loud bell rang, interrupting my thoughts.

"Lunchtime," Faith announced.

He guided me to the refectory, where students had already gathered. A prefect stood at the front and instructed someone to lead the prayer before we ate. The familiarity of that ritual was comforting.

Lunch that day was beans. I took my time eating, but after about twenty minutes, another bell rang. To my surprise, students immediately got up, clearing their trays. I barely made it halfway through my meal.

"You have to eat faster next time," Faith advised with a chuckle.

I sighed. I had never been in a boarding school before, and the rigid routine was new to me. I made a mental note to pick up the pace at dinner.

Two hours later, another bell rang. "That's for 'sister period,'" Faith said casually.

I blinked. "Sister period?"

He laughed at my confusion. "You'll see."

Later that evening, yet another bell signaled dinner. This time, we had rice, and I made sure to eat faster. After the meal,

Faith decided to introduce me to some of his friends from other hostels.

I was eager to meet them. I wanted to hear their stories, to understand how they had adjusted to life with visual impairment. That night, I listened intently as several students shared their journeys—how they lost their sight, how they coped, and the challenges they had overcome. Their words were filled with pain, resilience, and determination.

There was something deeply humbling about hearing their experiences. I had spent so much time focusing on what I had lost that I never considered what I could gain.

I didn't get to meet any of the female students, though—rules forbade boys from crossing into their hostel at night, and vice versa.

By 9 P.M., another bell rang. This time, it was for night prayers. We gathered at the assembly ground, sang hymns, and prayed. There was something powerful about the collective voices rising in unison, a reminder that even in darkness, faith could light the way.

That night, I slept like a newborn, my mind brimming with all I had seen, heard, and learned.

At 5:30 A.M., the bell rang again—morning prayers.

After the 20-minute session, we headed to the bathrooms behind the hostel for our showers. By the time we finished dressing, the 7 A.M. bell rang for breakfast. That morning, we had tea and bread, and for the first time since arriving, I felt a sense of belonging.

At 7:30 A.M., another bell rang—this time for the morning assembly. As we stood in neat lines, the principal addressed the school. Then, to my surprise, he introduced me as the newest student. A ripple of murmurs passed through the crowd, and I felt a swell of pride.

The school was structured into two sections: the Braille class and the regular class.

The Braille class was designed for students like me—those who had lost their sight after attending mainstream schools. It was a rehabilitation program meant to equip us with essential skills like reading and writing Braille, typing on a typewriter, and even learning how to operate a computer—though there were none available during my time. The program typically lasted two years, but those who mastered the skills sooner could leave early.

The regular class, on the other hand, was for students who had never been to a mainstream school. Most of them had been born blind or lost their sight early in life. They started by learning Braille and typing before progressing through primary education. Depending on when they started, they could spend up to six years in the program before transitioning to a secondary school.

As I stood there, listening to the principal's words, I felt something shift within me.

I had arrived uncertain, anxious, and full of fear. But now, for the first time in a long while, I felt something different—hope.

There was a new journey ahead of me, one that I had never anticipated. And as I looked around at my new classmates, I knew I wasn't walking it alone.

My First Classroom Experience as a Blind Person

A New Beginning: Embracing the Challenge with Joy

This special school, though struggling with limited funding and modest facilities, was powered by an unshakable spirit—a dedicated staff who poured their hearts into making the best of what they had. And honestly, that passion was contagious. Stepping into the classroom for the first time as a blind student was like stepping onto a thrilling, uncharted path. My heart pounded with excitement and a touch of nervousness. The familiar hum of voices, the rhythmic scrape of chairs, and the occasional burst of laughter filled the air. Without sight, every sound felt richer, more alive, painting an invisible yet vivid picture of my new world. As I found my seat, a rush of independence mixed with a newfound challenge surged through me—this was the beginning of something incredible.

The Braille class was divided into two sections: Class A and Class B. I was placed in Class A, alongside nine other students. Our teacher, Mr. Okey, was a soft-spoken, middle-aged man with a warmth that instantly put me at ease. He was also blind, yet his confidence and mastery over his surroundings were nothing short of inspiring. He welcomed me like an old friend and assured me that I would not only survive in his class but thrive. His encouragement felt like a gentle hand guiding me forward.

And so, my journey into the world of Braille began. Mr. Okey started with a captivating history of Braille—how a young boy named Louis Braille transformed six tiny dots into a gateway of knowledge and literacy for the blind. I hung onto every word, marveling at the ingenuity behind it. Then came the hands-on part. As my fingers traced the raised dots on the thick paper, trying to make sense of the patterns, it felt like unlocking a secret code—one that, once mastered, would open endless doors.

Letter by letter, dot by dot, we learned the Braille alphabet, both individually and in combination. It was like learning to read all over again, only this time, with my fingertips as my eyes. At the end of the lesson, Mr. Okey gave us our first assignment: memorize the dots and their corresponding letters. The challenge excited me.

That day, I met new friends, each navigating their own journey into this unfamiliar world. One of them was John, a kind-hearted and caring guy who was partially sighted. Though he couldn't read printed text, he was a tremendous help to those of us who were totally blind. He guided me and others to our next class—typewriting, which was in another building.

The typewriting class, though interesting, didn't spark the same level of awe as Braille had. I had seen a typewriter before when I had my sight, so it wasn't entirely new. But then, a curious thought struck me. *When I could see, I never even had the chance to touch a typewriter. Now that I'm blind, not only am I touching it—I'm owning it! I'm learning to operate it!* The irony wasn't lost on me, and rather than feeling down about it, I embraced the moment with gratitude.

After typewriting, we moved to our final class of the day—mobility and orientation. This class was a game-changer. We were taught the fundamentals of independent movement: how to use a mobility cane with confidence, the proper way to hold onto someone guiding us, how to enter a bus or car smoothly, how to locate and sit on a chair without fumbling, and, most importantly, how to interact with the world around us. It was an eye-opening experience—pun intended!

By the time we returned to the hostel, I was overflowing with joy. Something inside me had shifted. I no longer felt like a victim of my circumstances—I felt empowered, ready to take charge of my life. That night, John and I made a pact: we wouldn't spend more than a year in this school. Given our age and the long road ahead, we were determined to push ourselves, learn fast, and move forward.

With this resolve, we got to work. That evening, we enlisted some of the junior students, sweetening the deal with little treats, and convinced them to tutor us every evening after class. My friend Faith and the new companions we made also rallied behind us, offering help wherever they could. With determination, support, and, most importantly, the grace of God, something incredible happened—within two months, I could read and write Braille and type on the typewriter! My speed still needed work, but the progress was undeniable.

Every day at that school felt like unlocking a new piece of my potential. What had once seemed daunting had become exhilarating. I was learning, growing, and, for the first time in a long while, looking forward to the future with hope.

A Lesson in Perspective

During this period, something happened that still makes me laugh whenever I think about it. It was the Christmas season, and the school was organizing a Christmas carol. Due to our exceptional performance, my friend John and I were selected to read from the Braille Bible during the carol. I felt deeply honored by this opportunity.

Each of us was given Braille copy of the Bible chapters and verses we were assigned to read, and we were instructed to practice before the event. Eager to start, I settled on my bed that night, excitement burning within me as I began feeling the Braille dots on the paper.

However, as I started moving my fingers over the dots, everything felt strange, as if I had never touched Braille before. The more I tried to decipher the dots, the more confused I became. It all felt like a blocky, convoluted mess of dots that didn't make any sense. Before I knew it, I was sweating and my heart was pounding. I remembered the confidence my teachers had in me and all the accolades I had received for my quick learning.

Listening carefully, I could hear my friend John reading his passage correctly, along with others in the room. Not wanting anyone to know I was struggling, I kept quiet. Eventually, I fell asleep with the paper on my stomach, still anxious.

Later that evening, a friend from another room visited me. When he came to my bed, he touched the paper on my stomach and began reading it. Hearing this, I woke up. Realizing he was reading my paper, I quickly asked him to stop. Then, I asked him to start reading again, telling him I wanted to observe how he positioned his fingers. Stylishly, I traced his fingers as he read and soon discovered my mistake—I had turned the paper upside down. No wonder everything had seemed diagonal and meaningless.

Relieved and happy, I resumed practicing. This experience, as funny as it was, taught me a valuable lesson:

excitement can trip us up, but staying calm and double-checking can turn confusion into clarity. When things seem off, don't panic—verify your steps and ask for help if needed. Struggling alone in frustration often makes things worse; seeking assistance can provide the solution you need.

After this, I began to enjoy a great deal of independence and mastery. I could wash and iron my clothes, fetch water from the tap outside the hostel, and wash my plates—tasks my mom and siblings never let me do at home.

When the day of the carol finally came, my friend John and I exceeded everyone's expectations, especially considering how new we were. We were the best, and the whole school was super impressed and appreciated us a lot. From that moment on, we became popular in the school. But we never let our popularity derail our ambition and determination to graduate within one year. Everything was moving well for me.

Not long after, my mother visited and was shocked to see younger students with visual impairments. Seeing me and others manage so well had a healing effect on her. She was more encouraged than ever. The next time she visited, she brought my father and two siblings. They were all glad to see there was still hope and a great future for me.

My First Letter to Papa

During my mom's last visit, I decided to surprise my dad with a letter I typed on my typewriter. As I typed each word, I could feel the excitement building within me. When my father received the letter, his joy was unmistakable. He was not only delighted but also filled with gratitude to God for my growth and progress. The letter was more than just words on paper; it was a testimony to how far I had come, and it filled my dad with pride and hope for the future.

I Graduated in Eight Months instead of Two Years

Due to our stellar performance, beyond everyone's expectations, John and I were included among those graduating that session, even though we had not completed the required years. Out of the two years, we only spent eight months before achieving all we wanted. By this time, I could type, read, and write Braille perfectly. I knew I was no longer where I used to be. I had taken a significant step forward toward success. I thank God that my determination, resilience, and hard work paid off. Above all, God's grace was sufficient for me.

At the end of the session, John came first, and I came second in the whole class. On the day of our graduation, my family came. It was a healing, comforting, and joyful event.

Chapter 7:
THE CALL THAT CHANGED EVERYTHING

Prayer is one of the greatest mysteries of faith—an invisible conversation with an all-powerful God who hears even the faintest whisper of our hearts. Sometimes, His answers come like a gentle nudge, a quiet unfolding of events. Other times, they arrive in an overwhelming rush, so swift and precise that we are left breathless in awe. I had come to realize that while God's timing is beyond human understanding, His movement is always unmistakable—His hand orchestrates events in ways far beyond human comprehension. And I was about to witness this firsthand.

Before I lost my sight, I was in Junior Secondary Three, filled with the hopes and dreams of a young student eager to conquer the world. But all of that came to an abrupt halt. My education was cut short, and for a time, uncertainty and fear loomed over me like a dark cloud. Would I ever move forward? Would I ever reclaim a sense of purpose? These thoughts haunted me.

Though, after my time at the special school, something had shifted within me. No longer did I feel like a helpless boy trapped in an endless night. I had been equipped with tools that didn't just help me survive—they empowered me to thrive. The Braille Bible and books became my new gateway to knowledge, my stylus and Braille paper my means of written expression. Morse code offered me a secret language, and my typewriter allowed me to bridge the gap between my world and that of the sighted. My guide cane, once a symbol of limitation, had now become my silent but unwavering companion, leading me to freedom.

For the first time since losing my sight, I felt in control of my own life. I proved this to myself—and to others—when I visited my uncle and his family alone. Their stunned faces… well, I didn't see them, but I could tell from their voices and body language. Did I see that too? You better not argue with me—I *felt* it. Their reactions were priceless. 'Chidi, you came here by yourself?' My uncle's voice was thick with disbelief.

I could hear my aunt whispering a prayer of thanks. That moment filled me with an unspeakable sense of achievement.

But even with my newfound independence, one question still lingered: What next? I had conquered the fear of blindness, but now I stood at the edge of an unknown future. Should I return to complete my secondary education? Should I attempt higher studies? My heart longed for more, but reality was a stubborn obstacle. My parents couldn't afford the costly assistive technologies—computers, digital recorders, scanners—that would make learning easier for me. With three of my elder siblings already in school, the financial burden was simply too much. Still, I refused to let uncertainty paralyze me. Instead, I turned to the One who had been my strength through every trial—God.

A three-day fasting and prayer program was coming up in our church, and I knew this was my opportunity. I poured my heart out in prayer, seeking divine direction. My entire church family joined me, lifting their voices in intercession. I had no idea what to expect, but I believed in the power of prayer. And then, something extraordinary happened. On the final day of the fast, just as we were breaking it, my cousin arrived unexpectedly, holding out a phone. "Chidi, my brother's wife in Lagos wants to speak with you," he said. I was taken aback. Even before losing my sight, I had rarely spoken to the woman in question. Why was she calling me now? Her voice came through the receiver, warm and full of kindness. She sympathized with my condition, and then told me something that made my heart race.

She had discovered a special school for the blind in Lagos, located near her new business. As she observed the students there, she had been deeply impressed by the school's programs—computer training, music, soap-making, beadwork, and even sponsorship opportunities for students to further their education up to the university level. I felt a rush of emotions—shock, gratitude, and wonder.

This was no coincidence. It was the hand of God at work, a divine response to my prayers. As he spoke, a verse from Isaiah 42:16 flooded my heart: *"I will lead the blind by ways they have not known, along unfamiliar paths I will guide them; I will turn the darkness into light before them and make the rough places smooth."* This was it—God was leading me.

Without a second thought, I blurted out my interest, my voice trembling with excitement. Was this real? Could it really be happening? But, of course, I needed to speak with my parents first. I promised to give her an answer the next day. As I ended the call, I just sat there—stunned, overwhelmed, *and breathless.* Hours ago, I had been praying—pleading—for direction, unsure of what the future held. And now? God had answered, not in a whisper, not in a slow, uncertain process, but in a swift, undeniable move. The weight of uncertainty lifted, replaced by an electrifying realization—*a new chapter of my life was about to begin!*

When I shared the news with my family, the entire house buzzed with excitement. Lagos! The most developed city in Nigeria! The idea of moving there alone was exhilarating, but what thrilled me even more was what the school had to offer. Computers. Musical instruments. Real training in skills I had *longed* to learn. My previous school, as grateful as I was for it, had lacked many of these resources. This opportunity was beyond what I had dared to imagine.

That night, we gathered for a family meeting. The decision was unanimous—I was going to Lagos! But then came the first challenge: *money.* Lagos was far—*as far as the east is from the west.* And I mean that *literally.* Lagos sits in the western part of Nigeria, while Aba, in Abia State, is deep in the east, in the heart of Igbo land. The transportation costs for two were more than we could afford at the time. But we wouldn't let that stop us—not when an opportunity like this was on the line. Even if it meant borrowing, we were prepared to make it happen.

Just as worry began to creep in, another miracle unfolded. My uncle and his wife called again—almost as if they had been *listening to our conversation in real time.* Without hesitation, they offered to cover the transport expenses. Just like that, another barrier was *shattered.*

The days leading up to my departure were a blur of excitement, anticipation, and last-minute preparations. Then, finally, the day arrived. My eldest brother, Victor, and I set off for Lagos, embarking on an *11-hour journey* that tested both our patience and endurance. The roads were rough, the traffic was frustrating, and at some point, I was convinced we were going in circles. But none of that mattered—I was fueled by an unstoppable sense of *hope and adventure.*

By 4 a.m., we finally rolled into Lagos, weary from the long journey yet victorious in spirit. The city's early morning air was thick with the scent of damp earth and distant exhaust fumes, a stark contrast to the quiet towns we had passed. Waiting for us at the terminal, my uncle and his wife welcomed us with open arms, their voices brimming with warmth and reassurance.

After a much-needed rest, the next morning dawned with a sense of purpose. They guided us to the special school—the place I had envisioned in my prayers and dreams. As we stepped through its gates, a wave of emotions surged through me. The enrollment process felt surreal, each signature and stamped document sealing my fate. And then, it was official—I was now a student at the very institution that had once seemed like an impossible dream!

As if the day hadn't been magical enough, that evening, my uncle handed me a small box. I opened it, and there it was— *a brand-new phone.* My very first. My fingers ran over the smooth surface, my heart swelling with gratitude. This journey— this incredible, unpredictable, divinely orchestrated journey— was unfolding in ways I never could have foreseen. And I couldn't wait to see what came next.

Bethesda

The next morning, my dream became reality—I was officially a student at Bethesda! The moment I stepped onto the school grounds, I was thrilled. This wasn't just a school; it was a place of transformation, a sanctuary of hope. Owned by a remarkable woman with a heart of gold, Bethesda offered everything for free—food, accommodation, and invaluable education—all made possible by the generosity of donors in this vibrant, bustling city.

I could hardly believe I had come this far. Lagos—this city of endless possibilities—felt like a world away from everywhere I had ever been. It was overwhelming yet exhilarating. My heart swelled with gratitude, knowing that God had guided every step of my journey. Though I missed my hometown, especially my family, I found comfort in the company of students and staff who had walked similar paths. They understood, in ways others couldn't, what it meant to adapt, to fight for a future that once seemed out of reach. And knowing my uncle's family wasn't too far away made the transition even easier—they became a familiar thread in this new tapestry of my life.

Bethesda itself was humble but full of purpose. Nestled within a church compound, the school had only three rooms, each playing a vital role in shaping our education. The first was a multi-purpose space where we immersed ourselves in computer lessons, Braille reading and writing, and even music classes. It was a tight squeeze, but that hardly mattered—every moment inside those walls felt like an opportunity to learn something new. The second room was a workshop of creativity, where skilled hands crafted woven bags and beaded vases, turning simple materials into works of art. The third room belonged to the proprietress, the woman who had made all of this possible with her vision and dedication.

Though my previous school had more space and staff, Bethesda had something unique—modern teaching tools that unlocked new worlds for me. For the first time, I encountered musical equipment and computers, tools I had only imagined before. The moment I laid my hands on a bass guitar, something inside me stirred. I decided, right then and there, that I would learn to play it. The thought of mastering an instrument excited me beyond words—I could almost hear the deep, rhythmic notes vibrating through my fingertips.

Life at Bethesda was different in more ways than one. The students here weren't just my peers—they were my elders, many in their 40s and 50s. I felt like the youngest in the room, a surprising contrast to what I had expected from life in Lagos. Our living arrangements were also different. Instead of a dormitory, we stayed in a three-bedroom apartment two streets away from the school. The proprietress and her family occupied two rooms, while the female students shared the third. The male students, including me, made do with the living room and, on some nights, the balcony under the open sky. Space was tight, but I refused to be discouraged. I knew this was only a stepping stone, a place to grow before my journey carried me even further.

And then, something truly magical happened—I discovered that I could still play soccer!

Soccer had once been my greatest passion, but when I lost my sight, I thought I had lost the game forever. I had long since pushed away the ache of that loss, convincing myself it was part of the past. But then, to my utter amazement, I found out that blind people could still play! The moment I realized this, a fire reignited in me, a long-buried spark bursting into an uncontrollable flame. As I stepped onto the field once more, my heart pounded—not with fear, but with sheer, uncontainable joy. The ball had a special sound that guided us, and the thrill of the game came rushing back, stronger than ever. It was more than just a sport—it was a piece of myself that I had thought was gone forever, now restored.

As I settled into my new life, Bethesda became more than just a school—it became a home. The proprietress, her family, and the students embraced me with open arms. Despite the age differences, I quickly bonded with the older students, who shared their stories, their struggles, and their victories with me. Their wisdom became my guide, their experiences my lessons. Every conversation, every challenge, every discovery deepened my sense of belonging.

Bethesda wasn't just a stop along the way—it was the place where I learned to dream bigger, to embrace new possibilities, and to believe, more than ever, that my story was just beginning.

My Night Dreams

Not long after settling into my new environment, I began having a series of strange yet vivid dreams. In the first, I found myself at the front of a procession, confidently leading a group of blind students. The following night, I was handing out loaves of bread and fresh fruits to them, as if I were providing nourishment beyond just food. Then came the third dream—I was carrying a heavy bucket of water, ensuring my fellow students had enough to drink.

The dreams felt more than just random flickers of the mind; they carried a meaning I couldn't quite grasp. Their repetition made them impossible to ignore. I shared them with my father, who listened intently before offering his wise counsel. "Pray about it, my son," he said. "Stay focused. God might be revealing something special about your purpose in this school." His words lingered in my heart, stirring both curiosity and anticipation.

About a week later, the proprietress called me aside, her expression warm yet serious. I had no idea that what she was about to share would leave an indelible mark on my heart.

With a gentle smile, she began recounting her incredible journey. She told me about her two blind brothers and how, after she got married, her husband's blind sister became part of their home. As time passed, word spread about their kindness, and more families, desperate for help, started bringing their blind relatives to them. Their small home quickly became overcrowded, and financial struggles loomed over them like a dark cloud.

Determined to find a way forward, she and her family made the bold decision to move to Lagos, even though they had almost nothing. With no other options, they resorted to begging at a park. Just when it seemed like hope was slipping away, a pastor, deeply moved by their plight, offered them a place to stay in his church. They embraced the opportunity and began using music as a means of drawing support. Their heartfelt performances attracted donations, enabling them to rent a small apartment nearby. Before long, the church itself became more than just a shelter—it transformed into a school.

Slowly but surely, things started falling into place. They gathered educational materials, and support trickled in from local churches. Then, in what felt like a miraculous turn of events, the governor of Lagos State himself took notice. He celebrated his birthday at their school, and as a symbol of his support, he gifted them a brand-new bus.

As she spoke, I was completely captivated. Her story wasn't just inspiring—it was proof of resilience, faith, and the power of unwavering determination.

After sharing her incredible story, she leaned in and confided something that sent shivers down my spine—she had been watching me ever since I arrived. "God brought you here for a great and glorious purpose," she said, her voice filled with conviction. My heart pounded. Could this be connected to my dreams? My father's words echoed in my mind.

Then she revealed something I hadn't fully grasped: most of the people in the home were elderly blind individuals who had been with her since the beginning. But now, she had a new vision—a bold one. She wanted to transform the home into a place of learning, where blind students could receive a full education, from primary school to university. But for this dream to take shape, she needed young, determined students. And then came the shock—she wanted *me* to lead this transition.

I could barely process what was happening before she sprang into action. Within days, she had bought me a brand-new phone and laptop. My uncle had previously given me a phone, but it was almost useless to me—it didn't support screen reader software for the blind. But this one did. And she didn't stop there. She hired and paid a software engineer to install the necessary programs, making both the phone and laptop fully accessible.

I was stunned. In what felt like the blink of an eye, my life had taken a drastic, unexpected turn. One moment, I was just another student. The next, I had been entrusted with a mission far bigger than myself—one that could change lives.

To whom much is given, much is expected. That truth weighed heavily on me. Mummy—our beloved proprietor—had placed her trust in me, and I couldn't afford to fail her.

Without wasting time, I sprang into action. I reached out to my friends from my former special school, sharing the incredible opportunities our school was offering, including scholarships. Their enthusiasm was contagious! Not only were they eager to join, but they also helped spread the word, reaching out to others who might be interested.

And then, the miracle unfolded. Within just three weeks, over *twenty* students arrived, each one bringing renewed energy and purpose. The once-quiet home transformed into a lively learning hub. Coaching classes were set up, and academic lessons kicked off in full swing.

Mummy, ever the visionary, had no trouble recruiting teachers—qualified educators seemed to appear just when we needed them, as if divinely orchestrated. Watching the school evolve so rapidly was nothing short of breathtaking. I still couldn't believe that God had used *me* to make it happen.

Every time Mummy saw me, she couldn't stop smiling. "This is beyond what I imagined," she would say, her voice full of wonder. And honestly, I felt the same way. Everything had fallen into place with such ease—it was as if heaven itself had aligned to make it happen.

A few weeks later, Mummy called me in again. This time, she had a new assignment in mind.

"The school is flourishing," I could sense her saying it with a smile. "Now, we need a student captain."

My heart sank. I knew exactly where this was going. She wanted *me* to take the role.

Fear gripped me. Me? A leader? The thought alone was terrifying. I had always been shy—someone who avoided the spotlight, who preferred to blend into the background rather than stand before a crowd. But a school captain? That was *far* beyond me. It meant speaking on behalf of the school, representing us at events, addressing students... things I had never imagined myself doing.

I wasn't ready. I *didn't* want it.

There were other students—bold, confident, outspoken. Brilliant minds who could easily command attention. Surely, *one of them* would be a better fit.

Determined to dodge the responsibility, I came up with what I thought was the perfect escape plan. "Mummy," I suggested carefully, "why don't we let the students decide? Let's hold an election and allow them to choose their leader."

She considered it for a moment, then nodded. "That's a great idea."

I sighed in relief. *Perfect.* Someone else would be chosen, and I could go back to focusing on my education, my computer lessons, and my quiet life.

But life had other plans.

On election day, as the votes were tallied, I watched in stunned disbelief. Out of the three candidates, I won—*by a landslide.* A staggering *90%* of the votes.

Before I could fully process what had just happened, I was being sworn in as the president of the school.

I hadn't chosen leadership. It had chosen me.

And deep down, I knew—this was God's doing.

At that moment, it all started to make sense. The words my father had spoken to my mother that bleak night—when she was desperately grasping for hope—were coming to life right before my eyes.

The election had taken place on a Saturday, and by Sunday, we were scheduled to minister in a large church. That evening, Mummy called me aside.

"Our ministration tomorrow is important," she said, her voice calm but firm. "We need to deliver an *appealing and convincing* speech—something that will move people's hearts and stir them to respond to our needs."

Then, she held my hand. "You will be the one to speak."

I felt the weight of those words settle heavily on my chest. *Me? Speak? Before an entire congregation?*

That night, as I lay in bed, sleep refused to come. My mind raced with anxious thoughts. I had never stood before a crowd to give a speech. My vocabulary wasn't polished. I was still just a shy boy who preferred silence over speaking. How was I supposed to inspire an entire congregation?

But there was no escape. The responsibility had been placed squarely on my shoulders, and I *could not* fail.

In desperation, I turned to God.

"Lord," I whispered into the darkness, "please, fill my mouth with words."

As I prayed, a story from the Bible surfaced in my mind—the story of the blind man.

I recalled how the disciples had asked Jesus, *'Who sinned, this man or his parents, that he was born blind?'*

And I remembered Jesus' response: *'Neither this man nor his parents sinned, but that the works of God should be revealed in him.'*

The words struck a deep chord within me.

Could it be that my blindness—our blindness—was not a tragedy, but a testimony? A way for God's glory to be revealed?

But how could I take this ancient story and weave it into the reality of our lives? How could I make the congregation see *us* in that blind man—help them understand their role in revealing God's glory?

I didn't have the answers yet. But one thing was certain—this was bigger than me.

After much reflection, I came to a profound realization. Yes, we faced the undeniable struggles of blindness—the daily challenges, the unspoken fears—but there was something far greater at work. We were learning. We were growing. We could still return to school, operate computers and smartphones, and even play musical instruments. The absence of sight had not meant the absence of purpose. The glory of God *was* being revealed in our lives—just in a way most people never expected.

The next day, the moment arrived.

Our ministration electrified the entire church. The melodies soared, filling the sanctuary with a presence that was almost tangible. It was more than a performance—it was a revelation.

Then, it was my turn.

Taking a deep breath, I stepped forward, my heart pounding in my chest. I could feel the weight of a thousand eyes on me.

With gratitude, I began.

I thanked the congregation for their warm invitation, calling them a beacon of hope in what had once been the dark and desolate midnight of our journey.

Then, without hesitation, I spoke the words that had stirred my heart the night before.

I reminded them of Jesus' encounter with the blind man, of how His disciples had questioned whether sin had caused his condition. And I echoed Jesus' powerful response:

"Neither this man nor his parents sinned, but that the works of God should be revealed in him."

I paused, letting the words settle over the congregation.

"That same glory," I continued, "is still being revealed today—through us."

I spoke of how, despite our blindness, we could still learn, create, and thrive. I pointed to the ministration they had just witnessed—the harmonies that had filled the room, the skills we had honed, the technology we had mastered—all evidence that we were not bound by our limitations.

Then, I turned the focus back to them.

I reminded them of their sacred duty as the body of Christ—to comfort the brokenhearted, to feed the hungry, to clothe the naked, to be a refuge for those in need. And I told them that the glory of God, already shining in our lives, could only grow brighter with their kindness, their generosity, and their willingness to walk this journey with us.

As I spoke, I could feel something shifting in the atmosphere.

I assured them that their support would not be in vain—that with their help, we would rise, succeed, and defy the odds.

Then, silence.

And suddenly—applause.

Thunderous, overwhelming applause. It swelled around me, wave after wave, rolling through the church like a mighty current. At first, I thought it was for someone else. Surely, it couldn't be for me.

But it was.

The response was unlike anything in the history of the home. People weren't just clapping—they were moved. Many were weeping. The impact of our story, our faith, had reached them in a way I had never imagined.

When we returned home, Mummy was ecstatic. She embraced me with so much warmth, congratulating me over and over again.

"Chidi," she said, her voice thick with emotion, "your speech was powerful. Many people were crying while you spoke. You moved them."

Even my fellow students were in awe, surrounding me with words of admiration.

I had stepped into a moment I once feared. And by God's grace, I had not failed.

Chapter 8:
MY JOURNEY TO THE UNIVERSITY AND BEYOND

With every speech I delivered and every student I mentored, my confidence grew. I felt prepared—ready to take on the challenge of my Senior Secondary Certificate Examination (SSCE). But readiness does not always guarantee immediate success.

Despite my efforts, I faced setbacks. My first attempts at the SSCE did not go as planned, but I refused to be discouraged. In 2013, I tried again. By God's grace, I passed all my papers.

That same year, filled with hope, I sat for the UTME, only to fall short of the required 200-mark cutoff, scoring 180. Disappointed but undeterred, I tried again the following year—only to face the same result.

When I discovered that my score was enough to gain admission into a College of Education, I had a decision to make: stay back and try again for the university or move forward with what I had. I chose not to waste another year. I would go to college and keep striving for my university dreams.

But not everyone agreed with my decision. Mummy, our ever-supportive proprietor, was particularly unhappy. She believed I should wait, that another shot at the UTME would land me in my desired university. She reminded me of how much I meant to the school, how my absence would leave a vacuum. And, perhaps, deep down, she feared what awaited me in a new and distant place.

Understanding her concerns, I, too, felt a deep attachment to the school that had transformed my life. The thought of leaving a place where I had found purpose, growth, and a sense of belonging weighed heavily on me. But alongside that attachment was the gnawing uncertainty of my future. How long would I keep waiting for the perfect opportunity? What if another year still didn't get me into the university?

Torn between following my heart and securing my future, I wrestled with the decision. When Mummy saw that my mind was set on attending the college, she made one last attempt to dissuade me—this time with a firm threat: she would not sponsor my education.

I knew she wasn't being harsh out of malice; she genuinely believed I was making the wrong choice. But I also knew that if I backed down now, I might regret it forever. So, I took a different approach. The next day, I calmly informed her that my uncle had agreed to sponsor my education.

It was a gamble. And it worked.

Concerned about losing her influence over me, Mummy quickly changed her stance. With a sigh, she told me she would cover my expenses after all. It wasn't just about financial support—it was her way of letting me go, even if reluctantly.

With her blessing, I purchased the admission form for the Federal College of Education (Special), Oyo—an institution unlike any other in West Africa, designed for students with disabilities. The admission process went smoothly, and before I knew it, I was officially a student.

As my departure day approached, I stood at the threshold of a new beginning. Saying goodbye to the school was harder than I expected. Every corridor, every familiar voice, every moment I had spent there had shaped me. But the road ahead called me forward. With a heart full of gratitude and anticipation, I embraced this new chapter—the journey of integrating into mainstream society.

At the college, I was thrilled to be in an environment filled with non-disabled peers. It was a new kind of integration—one I had longed for. The college, designed to train students to care for and educate individuals with disabilities, felt both welcoming and familiar. Yet, the real excitement lay in the little things—like the independence of cooking for myself, something I had always wanted to master.

Choosing to study English, I hoped to sharpen my vocabulary and refine my communication skills. But beyond academics, what fascinated me most was the diversity of disabilities represented among students. From hearing impairments to intellectual and behavioral disorders, I saw firsthand the vast spectrum of human resilience. Attending mainstream classes again felt like stepping into a world I had once thought beyond my reach—a world where my disability did not define my limitations.

As my first year drew to a close, I decided to take another shot at the UTME. It was a leap of faith, but deep down, I hoped for a breakthrough. And then, near the end of the year, my phone rang. It was our proprietor. Her voice carried an excitement that sent my heart racing.

"Chidi, you scored 219!"

For a moment, I couldn't speak. I had not just passed—I had surpassed the 200-mark required for my dream university. The realization hit me all at once. I had done it. I was finally on my way to the University of Lagos.

Although I had enjoyed my time at the college, made wonderful friends, and grown in ways I never imagined, the prospect of attending one of Nigeria's most prestigious universities was exhilarating. After my second-semester exams, I began breaking the news to my friends. Taiwo, my girlfriend, was happy for me, though I could hear the sadness in her voice. My friends congratulated me, but the goodbyes were bittersweet. That night, I lay awake, reflecting on my time at the college. Every face, every conversation, every lesson—it had all shaped me. I would miss them. But this was my path, and I had to follow it.

Returning to Lagos felt like coming home. As I stepped into the special school, our proprietor and the students welcomed me with open arms. Their joy was infectious, and in that moment, I realized just how deeply my presence had mattered to them.

Then came the moment that changed everything—I received my official admission letter from the University of Lagos. Holding that letter in my hands, I felt a wave of emotions I could barely contain. I picked up my phone and dialed home.

"Papa, I got in."

There was silence on the other end, followed by a sound I never expected—my father, crying. His voice trembled as he spoke.

"The boy they once called useless... my son is going to university."

His words hit me like a flood, washing away years of struggle, doubt, and pain. And in that moment, a memory resurfaced—one that had haunted me for years.

When I lost my sight completely, a relative had made a shocking statement:

"Chidi is better off dead than living with blindness."

I knew he hadn't meant harm, but his perception—his finality—had been crushing, not just to me but to my entire family.

Yet here I was, standing on the threshold of a future that many thought impossible. I had proven them wrong—not just for myself, but for every person who had ever been told they wouldn't amount to anything.

As my fellow students and I completed our registration at the university, we made a pact to return to the special school on weekends—to stay connected to the place that had nurtured us. Then, the day finally came. With my bags packed and my heart full of anticipation, I stepped into the next chapter of my life.

The University of Lagos—one of the finest institutions in Nigeria—stood before me, waiting to embrace me into its world. And I was ready.

Choosing Sociology: My Motivation and Experiences

The decision to study sociology was not just an academic pursuit; it was a personal mission—one deeply rooted in my journey through the maze of discrimination, segregation, and stigmatization that many disabled individuals face. Society had often viewed people like me through the lens of limitation rather than potential, and I was determined to change that narrative. I longed to understand the intricate web of human relationships, the unspoken rules that governed interactions, and the systemic barriers that hindered inclusion. More than anything, I wanted to be part of the solution, to use knowledge as a tool to dismantle prejudice and build bridges of understanding.

Arriving at the University of Lagos was a moment of triumph, not just for me but for everyone who had ever dared to dream beyond the restrictions imposed upon them. As I stepped onto the sprawling campus, I was overwhelmed with a profound sense of accomplishment. The grandeur of the institution, its rich academic heritage, and the sheer magnitude of possibilities it held left me breathless. It was larger and more complex than any school I had ever attended, yet I felt an unshakable resolve—I belonged here, and I would make the most of this opportunity.

Despite the university's architectural brilliance, mobility posed a challenge. The absence of ramps and accessible pathways meant I often needed the guiding hands of friends. But rather than feeling frustrated, I embraced the reality with gratitude. Every challenge was a lesson, every obstacle an opportunity to rise above limitations. And I was never alone—compassionate souls seemed to find me at every turn. My presence attracted attention, not because I was extraordinary, but because God's grace had always gone ahead of me, opening doors, touching hearts, and providing exactly what I needed at the right time.

Support came in ways I had never imagined. My special school's proprietor, whose unwavering belief in me had been a pillar of strength, used her influence to secure three sponsors for my education. These generous benefactors, alongside my family and the proprietor herself, ensured that I could pursue my studies without the shadow of financial burden. Their kindness was proof of the power of goodwill, reminding me that no one succeeds alone.

Beyond academics, living independently was a dream realized. The simple joys of cooking my own meals, keeping my space in order, and navigating life without constant dependence were liberating. Each small victory—preparing a meal, finding my way to class, managing my affairs—was a celebration of resilience and growth.

I had come a long way, but the journey was far from over. Every lecture, every conversation, every experience at the University of Lagos was shaping me into the person I was destined to become. And for that, I was eternally grateful.

My Ideology about Giving

Friendship, to me, was never a one-sided affair. While my friends—both in the hostel and my department—extended their generosity towards me, I was determined to give back in every way I could. Giving was not about having an abundance of resources; it was about having a heart willing to share.

Though my room was designed for only two, it often became a sanctuary for classmates who needed a place to stay. At times, up to ten of us squeezed into that small space, yet the joy of togetherness made every inconvenience insignificant. To make them more comfortable, I bought a rug so those sleeping on the floor wouldn't have to endure the cold, hard tiles. I delighted in cooking for the group, and on days when I couldn't prepare meals myself, I made sure to provide the necessary food supplies.

Beyond the walls of our crowded room, my spirit of giving extended into other areas of my life. Whenever we went out, I covered transportation costs for friends, and for those who assisted me, I found ways to express my appreciation—whether through small gifts or thoughtful gestures. Giving, for me, was never about repaying a debt; it was a way of showing gratitude to both God and the wonderful people He had placed in my life.

More importantly, I wanted to challenge the notion that generosity is reserved for those with excess. My disability did not diminish my ability to give, nor did it define my worth. I firmly believed that a person's value is not measured solely by what they receive, but by the love, kindness, and support they extend to others. In sharing what I had, I wasn't just giving—I was affirming that everyone, regardless of their circumstances, has something meaningful to offer the world.

Challenges during Lectures

One of the greatest challenges I faced in university was keeping up with lectures when instructors relied heavily on visual teaching methods—writing on the board, drawing diagrams, or pointing to illustrations I couldn't see. As one of only three visually impaired students in my class, I often stood out—not just because of my disability, but because of my determination to excel.

Fortunately, my lecturers were understanding and made efforts to ensure that learning was accessible. Yet, the real challenge was not just in receiving information, but in processing, organizing, and making sense of it independently. Unlike my sighted peers who could jot down notes with ease, I relied on technology to bridge the gap.

I used speech software to navigate my studies, scanners to convert printed materials into digital text, and digital recorders to capture lectures. My laptop became my most valuable tool—I typed notes, completed assignments, and even wrote my exams and projects, later printing them with the help of a flash drive. The process was far from simple. Scanning documents, saving them on my computer, and then using a screen reader to study required patience and discipline. Yet, rather than feeling burdened by the extra effort, I found joy in it. The ability to harness technology was not just a means to an end—it was a source of empowerment, a testament to how far I had come.

Despite the hurdles, I thrived. My performance in exams often exceeded expectations, earning me a reputation as a highly intelligent student. I actively participated in class discussions, sharing insights that challenged perspectives and enriched conversations. This, in turn, earned me the respect of both my lecturers and peers.

Every obstacle I faced only reinforced my belief that limitations exist only where we allow them to. My success was not just a personal triumph; it was a message to others that with determination, perseverance, and the right tools, anything is possible.

Graduation and Reflection

At the end of my four-year journey at the University of Lagos, I walked away with more than just a degree—I carried with me a profound sense of triumph. Graduating with a Second Class Upper Division was more than an academic achievement; it was proof of resilience, perseverance, and the boundless power of faith and determination.

Looking back, I marveled at how far I had come—from the uncertainty of my early years to this moment of fulfillment. Education had not only illuminated my path but had also unearthed strengths, talents, and possibilities I had never imagined. It had empowered me to embrace my disability, not as a limitation, but as a unique perspective through which I could inspire, advocate, and transform challenges into stepping stones.

Every struggle, every late-night study session, and every moment of doubt had led to this victory. My journey was proof that no circumstance, no obstacle, and no voice of discouragement could define my potential. I had rewritten my story, not just for myself, but for everyone who had ever been told they couldn't succeed.

As I stood at the threshold of a new chapter, my heart swelled with gratitude—gratitude to God, to my family, to the teachers and friends who had walked this journey with me, and also to Mummy Chioma, my special school proprietress, and the sponsors.

The road ahead was unknown, but one thing was certain: I was ready. Armed with knowledge, faith, and an unyielding spirit, I stepped forward, eager to embrace the future.

Chapter 9:
MIRACULOUS ENCOUNTERS AND DIVINE PROTECTION

Life has a way of shifting in the blink of an eye. One moment, everything seems to be falling into place, and the next, you find yourself teetering on the edge of disaster. I had tasted triumph, defied the odds, and pushed past limitations, but lurking beneath these victories were moments when fate seemed to conspire against me—moments where a single misstep could have altered my story forever.

Yet, time and again, just when calamity seemed inevitable, an unseen hand intervened. The line between tragedy and survival was razor-thin, but by the mercy and grace of Almighty God, I walked away, not just unscathed, but victorious.

It happened on a day like any other. I was walking alone, my steps steady, my thoughts drifting, completely unaware that danger was racing toward me. A truck was speeding in my direction, its driver assuming, like any normal person would, that I could see him coming and would step aside. But I couldn't. My sight was failing me, and I had no idea that my life was hanging by a thread.

Then suddenly, chaos.

I heard it—people shouting, their voices rising with panic. They were warning me, screaming for me to move. But before my mind could catch up, before I could even react, something—some unseen force—shoved me with such power that I flew into a nearby gutter.

And then, silence.

The truck thundered past, missing me by inches. The people who had been watching stood frozen, their faces pale with shock. To them, I had just vanished under the massive tires, and they braced for the worst. Some even looked away, unable to bear what they thought they had just witnessed.

But then—just like in a dramatic movie scene—I climbed out of the gutter, not as a ghost, not as a broken man, but as a completely unharmed, very bewildered survivor.

The crowd gasped. Their expressions turned from horror to disbelief, as if they had just seen a miracle unfold before their eyes. At first, some of them scolded me, saying I had been careless, that I had nearly given them heart attacks. But when they found out I was losing my sight, their frustration softened into sympathy.

Yet I was the one left with the biggest questions: Who—or what—had pushed me? There was no one close enough to have done it. Was it an angel? A divine intervention? A mysterious helping hand that vanished as quickly as it appeared?

I may never fully understand what happened that day, but one thing is certain—it left me with wisdom that will stay with me forever. Life has a way of teaching lessons in the most unexpected ways, and that moment was no exception.

For one, not all dangers are visible. Some threats lurk just beyond our awareness, unseen yet no less real. But just because we don't see them doesn't mean they can't harm us. Time and again, divine grace shields us from perils we never even realize were there. Looking back, I now recognize that I was being protected from something far worse than I could have imagined.

Then, there's the way salvation sometimes comes—not as a gentle pull but as a forceful shove. We often expect God to guide us with a soft whisper, nudging us in the right direction, but sometimes, He pushes us—hard—into safety. In those moments, we may not understand why things happen the way they do, but later, we realize that the push was necessary.

What seemed like a setback at first turned out to be my saving grace. Landing in a gutter was hardly a dignified experience. In fact, at the time, it felt like a disgrace. But when I think about it now, that fall is the very thing that saved my life. So many times, what we perceive as a failure or a misfortune is actually God's way of repositioning us for something greater.

Of course, people are quick to judge before they understand. In those first few moments, I was scolded, assumed to be reckless and careless. No one stopped to ask what had actually happened. But the moment they heard the full story, their attitude shifted. It's a reminder that the world is often too eager to pass judgment, yet true understanding only comes with knowledge.

And through it all, one undeniable truth remains—miracles still happen. Whether it was an angel, an unseen hand, or just divine timing, I was saved in a way that defies explanation. And if that isn't proof of God's hand in our lives, I don't know what is.

That day, I walked away with more than just my life—I walked away with faith, wisdom, and a newfound appreciation for the way God moves in mysterious ways. And most importantly, I learned that sometimes, when life pushes you, it's not to hurt you—it's to save you.

A Miraculous Rescue: Saved by an Unseen Hand

Some moments in life are so surreal that even if you try to explain them, people just shake their heads and say, "Are you sure you weren't dreaming?" But I know what I saw—or rather, what I almost didn't see.

It happened during the same period when I still had some partial vision left—just enough to convince myself I could manage, but not enough to truly trust my eyes. That evening, I had gone to visit Mary, my love at the time. You know how young love is—every visit feels too short, every goodbye lingers longer than it should.

By the time I should have left, the rain had started. And not just any rain—July rain. The kind that falls relentlessly, drowning the streets in murky water, blurring the lines between road, sidewalk, and unseen dangers. I waited, hoping it would stop, but the rain had other plans. Darkness crept in, and with it, the realization that I could not risk walking home too late. Rain or no rain, I had to leave.

I stepped out into the flooded streets, my heart pounding a little faster than usual. My vision was failing me, but I pressed on, relying on memory and instinct to guide my steps. That's when it happened.

Ahead of me, hidden beneath the swirling floodwaters, was a deep pit. To me, the path seemed clear—just wet and slippery. I stepped forward, unaware that I was about to walk straight into disaster.

Then—out of nowhere—a man appeared.

I didn't hear him approach. I didn't see where he came from. All I know is that just as I was about to take the final step into the unknown, his hand shot out and grabbed me. With a firm pull, he yanked me backward, away from the pit. He said, I guess you are new to this area, there is a big ditch you're walking into" he calmly said.

For a moment, I just stood there, heart hammering, drenched from head to toe, trying to process what had just happened. I turned to thank him, to ask who he was, but all he said was, "Go."

And then, just like that, he was gone.

I don't know where he went. I don't know how he knew I was in danger. All I know is that if he hadn't been there at that exact moment, I wouldn't be telling you this story.

And that's when it hit me—this wasn't the first time I had been pulled back from the brink of disaster. The truck incident flashed through my mind. The unseen force that had shoved me into a gutter to save my life… Was it the same hand that had pulled me away from the pit? Was this man an angel? Had divine protection stepped in once again?

I believe with all my heart that I was never alone. Too many close calls, too many near misses—there's no way they were all just luck. I am convinced that Divine protection is real. Someone, somewhere, is always watching over me .

I also came to understand that not all saviors stay. Some people enter our lives for just a moment—to rescue us, to redirect us, to change our path—and then they disappear. Searching for them is futile. Instead, we should be grateful for their presence, however brief, and move forward.

Another lesson I learned is that life's greatest dangers are often the ones we don't see. The deepest pits aren't always physical holes in the ground but unseen traps—wrong decisions, bad influences, unforeseen consequences. And just like that night, we must trust that when we're about to fall, God will send help, even if it comes from a stranger.

And finally, when life's storms rage, when the path ahead is uncertain, and when danger lurks beneath the surface, remember this: Sometimes, God doesn't just walk beside us. Sometimes, He reaches out, grabs our arm at the last second, and pulls us back just in time.

A Brush with Disaster: The Miracle of an Intact Leg

By this time, my sight had completely faded. On one occasion, as I headed back to the special school after a holiday break, a female friend accompanied me to catch a cab. While we waited by the roadside to cross, a car approached and attempted to park near us. The driver overshot his mark, and before I knew it, the back tire rolled over my leg. Shocked and disoriented, I screamed in pain. My friend, realizing what had happened, started pounding on the car to get the driver's attention. The windows were rolled up, making it hard for him to hear. Only after she shouted at him to move forward did he finally do so.

The few moments when the tire was on my leg were filled with overwhelming fear. I thought my leg was shattered and that I might never walk again. Miraculously, when the tire was removed, I found my leg intact—no wounds, no bruises. Witnesses were stunned, and even my friend couldn't believe it. I felt only minor discomfort. When I stood up and walked without issue, I was in complete awe. The miracle of escaping such a potentially disastrous accident left me profoundly grateful.

As we waited for a cab on the other side of the road, I noticed my friend was still crying. I asked her why, given that I was unharmed. She expressed guilt, feeling that she hadn't acted quickly enough to warn me. Her tears moved me deeply. To comfort her, I reassured her that the accident wasn't her fault. I encouraged her to be grateful with me for the miracle of my safety. Her tears eventually subsided, and she apologized for her reaction. When a cab finally arrived, she offered to accompany me, but I declined to avoid further burdening her. I appreciated her support and reassured her of my safety. After this, she let me go, and I arrived home safely. When I shared the story with the matron and other students at the special school, they were in utter disbelief.

The Pushing Bus and the Busy Road

On another unforgettable occasion, I was returning from the university to the special school, my mind filled with the familiar anticipation of getting back to the safe, comforting environment I had grown to know so well. As I arrived at the school, a cab driver dropped me off right in front of the gates before quickly speeding away. Alone, I stood at the roadside, waiting for someone to assist me across to the entrance. The bustling traffic and the usual noise of the street were distant, but in that moment, it all seemed strangely quiet.

Without warning, a sudden shove from behind jolted me out of my thoughts. I turned in shock and realized I was standing directly behind a bus that had begun reversing, its massive form inching back toward me with no one at the wheel to see me. The bus driver, completely unaware of my presence, continued to reverse, pushing me dangerously close to the edge of the busy road. I felt an icy wave of fear wash over me as I stood frozen, only feet away from the speeding traffic that raced down the street. The danger felt too real, my heart pounding in my chest as I feared the worst.

But in that moment of terror, something beyond me happened. I felt an inexplicable, yet undeniable force push me away from the looming bus, guiding me toward safety. Time seemed to slow as I was propelled to the side, narrowly avoiding the chaos of the road. The shrill screams of bystanders echoed in the background, their alarm only amplifying the tension of those fleeting seconds. And then, just as suddenly as it had happened, I was safe. Unharmed, standing on the sidewalk, still reeling from what had just transpired.

That night, as I reflected on the harrowing incident, my heart swelled with gratitude and awe. How could I not marvel at the divine intervention that had spared my life? I had no explanation for how I had been saved—no reason other than God's grace. His protective hand had guided me when I couldn't see the danger, fulfilling His promise to lead the blind along unknown paths and turn darkness into light. I couldn't help but feel a profound sense of awe, knowing that even in the darkest of moments, He was always there, watching over me.

Stranded on the Highway

One of the most heart-stopping experiences I've ever had took place when I was traveling alone to an event. I had boarded a "Danfo" bus, the quintessential Lagos transportation experience—crowded, noisy, and often an adventure in itself. I had informed both the driver and conductor of my intended stop, trusting they would take me there safely. However, as we continued on the journey, something didn't feel right.

You see, by this time, I had completely lost my sight. So, I couldn't see the passing landmarks or tell where we were. I had to rely entirely on what others told me. And as the minutes ticked by, it became clear that something was wrong. At first, I thought I was just overthinking it, but when I asked the conductor where we were, I nearly lost my breath when he casually mentioned that we were on the flyover. *Wait—what?*

My heart sank. We were *on the flyover*, miles above the ground! Normally, that would've been a place where I'd be able to see everything around me, but all I had was the sound of the city whizzing by and the realization that I was nowhere near my stop. Panic immediately set in. *I told you where I needed to stop! Why are we here?* I almost screamed, but I just couldn't breathe in the chaos of it all. The conductor, sensing the urgency, asked the driver to stop. They finally let me out of the bus, but as soon as the door shut behind me, the driver sped off, leaving me standing alone on the edge of a busy highway.

Completely disoriented and not knowing where I was, I stood there, my mind racing. I could hear the hum of traffic around me, people rushing by, oblivious to my predicament. There was a brief moment of calm, where I felt the pavement under my feet. I simply froze, hoping that somehow I would be able to figure it all out. But standing there in complete uncertainty, the weight of being stranded in such a busy part of Lagos made my heart race even faster.

The fear and frustration took over, and I couldn't hold back the tears. I was scared, frustrated, and feeling utterly alone. I didn't know where I was, and no one seemed to notice me in the crowd. But then, in the midst of my panic, I remembered something: I had been in tight spots before, and every single time, God had pulled me through. So I closed my eyes, even though I couldn't see, and prayed. I thanked God for the times He had helped me in the past and asked for His guidance in that very moment. I had no choice but to trust.

Then, just when I thought all hope was lost, I heard footsteps approaching. I reached my hand out, unsure of who or what was coming, but there it was—a hand. A man's hand. At first, he seemed startled, but when I indicated that I was blind, everything clicked. His surprise turned to compassion, and without hesitation, he took my hand and led me away from the traffic.

He didn't stop there. He didn't just help me across the road and leave. No, this stranger went above and beyond. He arranged for another bus to take me to my destination. But the most extraordinary part was yet to come—he even walked me to the venue of the conference, ensuring I was safe and sound.

It wasn't until later, when I reflected on the entire experience, that I realized the true magnitude of what had happened. The man told me where I had been standing—a bridge, miles above the ground. He explained that most people don't walk on that part of the highway, let alone at that height. It hit me like a ton of bricks: What had brought him to that very place, at that precise time? Was it chance? Was it fate? Or was it God orchestrating everything perfectly, as He always does?

In that moment, I realized just how intricately God had worked to bring help exactly when I needed it. He had placed that man in the right place at the right time, just when I needed someone to guide me.

As the day went on, I couldn't stop reflecting on how God had seen me through yet another challenging moment. Despite the fear, despite the uncertainty, I had come out unscathed, once again a testimony of the unending grace and protection He offers. With unwavering faith, I had faced this challenge head-on and emerged victorious, proving to myself that no obstacle is too great when God is by your side.

I walked away from that day with a deep sense of gratitude and awe. It wasn't the adventure I'd planned, but it was a beautiful reminder that God's timing is always perfect. Even when we can't see, He's right there, guiding us, protecting us, and bringing us through. And that's a lesson I'll carry with me forever.

As I reflect on these experiences—these miraculous moments that saved my life—I am overwhelmed with gratitude for the unseen forces that protected me. Each encounter, whether it was a shove into a gutter, a pull from a pit, or a sudden push away from a reversing bus, has reaffirmed the profound truth that divine protection is always at work in ways we may never fully understand. The hand of God has intervened in my life time and again, not just to shield me from physical harm, but to teach me that we are never truly alone, even in our darkest moments.

Through these ordeals, I learned that life's challenges often disguise themselves as setbacks, and what feels like a fall is sometimes just a redirection toward something greater. I have come to realize that it's in our most vulnerable moments that God's presence shines brightest. His mercy doesn't always show up in the way we expect it. Sometimes, it's a sudden shove, a fleeting presence, or a quiet whisper guiding us back on course.

The lessons I've learned from these miraculous encounters go beyond gratitude. They remind me that faith is not just about believing in God's promises; it's about trusting that, no matter the storm, He will see us through to the other side. My life is proof of the power of divine protection and intervention. There is no doubt in my heart that the miracles I've experienced are not coincidences—they are signs of God's love and grace at work.

To anyone who feels lost, broken, or in the midst of a storm, I encourage you to keep going. Trust that even when you can't see the way ahead, there is a force greater than yourself guiding you, protecting you, and leading you toward safety. Sometimes, we don't need to understand why things happen the way they do—we just need to trust that we are being guided for a reason.

As I stand here today, not as a victim of blindness, but as a victor, I encourage you to look back at the miracles in your own life, no matter how small or seemingly insignificant they may seem. Recognize the divine presence that walks beside you and be grateful for the moments when life could have turned out differently, but didn't.

Miracles still happen. Divine protection is real. And we are never alone.

Chapter 10:
MY FAMILY AND SIGNIFICANT RELATIONSHIPS

As you may have gathered from my story so far, I am blessed with a wonderful family. It is often said that the family is the smallest unit of life, but I also believe it is the greatest. Without their love, care, and support, my faith would not have been as strong, nor would I have found the courage to navigate the darkest moments of my life. Though life's unpredictable circumstances took away my sight, I remain eternally grateful to God for the incredible family He blessed me with.

Family is the cornerstone of our lives—a foundation that provides unwavering support, especially during our most challenging moments. The bond we share with our loved ones offers a sense of belonging and security that nothing else can replace. My family played an invaluable role in my journey with blindness, standing by me with unconditional love. Their encouragement reminded me that, no matter how difficult the road ahead, I was never alone.

Growing up in a family of six children, being the fifth, I was surrounded by love on all sides. Though we didn't have the luxuries of life, we had something far greater—love in abundance. My parents, though not wealthy, showered us with care and attention, ensuring no child ever felt left out. There was no favoritism in our home; love was shared equally, and we, as siblings, always looked out for one another.

There are times I wonder how I could have endured the nagging and depressing ordeal of blindness without such a supportive family. At every step, they whispered words of encouragement, reassuring me that they were always with me. How could I not be comforted when I knew I had such a unique and wonderful family—one that refused to let me down, no matter how tough the journey got? Every day, I see my family as a divine gift, a blessing that sustains me. Though the gift of sight is gone, the dazzling light of family remains, becoming one of my greatest sources of strength, hope, and dignity.

From the very beginning of my visual impairment, my family has been there for me in every way—spiritually, emotionally, and even financially. I can still picture those early mornings when my father would walk into my room, encouraging me with the Word of God. My mother's loving eyes and outstretched hands guided me through the uncertainty, filling my heart with reassurance.

As I grappled with the emotional and psychological effects of blindness, I began to withdraw from society, isolating myself from others. My self-esteem plummeted, and I wanted nothing more than to disappear into my own world. But my siblings refused to let that happen. They made sure I was never alone, insisting that I join them wherever they went. Even when I tried to avoid their invitations, they knew how to nudge me along. They were never ashamed of my condition; instead, they took pride in introducing me to their friends and colleagues. Even those who were married wanted me to spend time with them, ensuring I always felt loved and included in their lives.

One of the greatest blessings in my life was when my sister got married and eventually relocated to Lagos. Some might see it as mere coincidence, but I see it as nothing short of a miracle—a divine intervention meant for me. Lagos, with its relentless pace, chaotic streets, and overwhelming crowds, is an incredibly difficult place for a visually impaired person to navigate. But having a family member who genuinely cared about me in such a city was unimaginable.

When she moved to Lagos, I was overjoyed. Suddenly, I had not only my uncle and his wife—the ones who had first brought me to Lagos—but also my sister Victoria. She became more than just a sister; she became my rock, my support system, my source of comfort in a city that could have otherwise swallowed me whole. Her kindness, patience, and unconditional love have been a lifeline, a constant reassurance that I am not alone. She has stood by me through thick and thin, always looking out for my well-being, making sure I never lacked care or companionship.

Victoria has been a tremendous help in more ways than I can count. She has not only provided me with a place of refuge but has also been a source of strength and encouragement. Whether it was guiding me through the unfamiliar streets of Lagos, ensuring I had everything I needed, or simply being a listening ear when I needed to talk, her presence in my life has been nothing short of a blessing.

It was a turn of events that I could never appreciate enough. The comfort and security she and her family brought into my life in Lagos were invaluable. With her around, I found courage in a city that once seemed daunting. Victoria's selflessness and unwavering support have shown me what true love and devotion look like.

Relationships and Support Systems

Relationships are the threads that weave the fabric of our lives, shaping who we are and guiding us through the journey of life. Whether it's the love of family, the enduring bond of friendship, or the mentorship that helps us grow, these connections are essential to our well-being and personal development. They enrich our lives with meaning, helping us navigate challenges and celebrate joys. In this passage, I will share the stories of remarkable individuals whose relationships profoundly impacted my life, shaping the person I am today.

Benjamin: My First and Truest friend

When I lost my sight, it felt like I had also lost the connections that once filled my life with warmth and joy. Friends who had been close gradually drifted away, their calls and visits becoming fewer until they stopped altogether. It was as if my blindness had created an invisible barrier between us, leaving me to navigate this new, challenging world largely on my own. But just when I felt most alone, Benjamin stepped into my life.

Benjamin, the brother of my uncle's wife, quickly became someone incredibly special to me. From the moment we met at my maternal home, he showed a genuine interest in getting to know me, and his presence became a source of comfort and companionship that I desperately needed. He made it his mission to ensure I never felt isolated, often taking me out to experience the world in a new way. Despite my blindness, he made me feel that I was still part of the vibrant life happening around me.

Our friendship soon deepened, and Benjamin began inviting me to his home, where his family welcomed me with open arms. His parents, siblings, and relatives embraced me as one of their own, filling a void that had grown in my heart since the loss of my sight. Their kindness and acceptance provided a sense of belonging that was both healing and uplifting.

Benjamin's devotion to me was unwavering. He moved beyond mere friendship, becoming a constant presence in my life. He even began staying with us at my uncle's place just to be close to me, showing a level of commitment and care that went far beyond what I had expected. Even after I moved away, Benjamin continued to visit regularly, proving that his friendship was not temporary but a lasting and true bond.

Through his actions, Benjamin demonstrated the power of true friendship. When others had turned away, he remained, filling the empty spaces in my life with his kindness, care, and unwavering support. His friendship reminded me that I was not walking this difficult path alone. Benjamin's presence

113

reinvigorated my spirit, giving me the strength to face the challenges ahead with renewed hope and confidence. He showed me that there are still good, kind-hearted people in this world, and for that, I will always be grateful.

Christian: I Call Him Dodo

At every turning point in my life, God has graced me with the presence of comforting angels disguised as friends. This time, that angel's name is Christian, though I lovingly call him Dodo. We first crossed paths at the second special school I attended, Bethesda, where, despite his partial sight, he could navigate the world around him, though reading print remained a challenge. From the very moment we met, an unbreakable bond formed between us, one that quickly blossomed into a deep and enduring friendship.

Christian became more than just a friend—he became my rock, my guide, my confidant. Whether inside the school or out in the bustling world, Christian was always by my side, offering his eyes to help me see the world more clearly. He would accompany me everywhere, ensuring I was never alone on my journeys. At the market, he would help me pick out clothes, making sure every detail was just right, down to my glasses being in perfect condition. His presence in my life was like a breath of fresh spring air, filling my world with warmth, care, and a sense of security I could always rely on.

When we both received admission to the university, our friendship only deepened. We shared a room and, more importantly, shared countless moments of laughter, support, and understanding. Christian's unwavering support was a lifeline during those university years. Even though his classes were in a different department, he never hesitated to walk me to lectures. After his own classes, he would check on me, help with my tasks, and make sure I was never alone in any of my endeavors.

Whether it was a trip to the market or a walk to church, Christian's companionship made the world feel less daunting and more like a place where I could thrive.

What made Christian's support so profound was his deep understanding of my struggles. With his own visual impairment, he knew the challenges I faced, and his empathy was a balm to my soul. He didn't just help me—he truly understood me, knowing exactly how to ease my burdens and make my life a little brighter. Through my time at Bethesda and the University of Lagos, Christian remained a constant source of strength, kindness, and unwavering support—a blessing I am endlessly grateful for.

Bro Eze: The Kindest Man Ever

Angels are scattered throughout our world, waiting to offer help to those in need, and I have been blessed to encounter several of them throughout my life's journey. During my national service at the Federal College of Education in Oyo State, I was graced with the presence of another extraordinary friend, Mr. Princewill, whom I fondly call "Bro Eze."

Like me, Bro Eze was blind from birth. Despite his own challenges, he stood out as one of the most empathetic, kind, and selfless individuals I have ever met. Although he was considerably older than I, our shared experience of blindness and our common tribal roots, which allowed us to speak the same language, forged a deep and immediate bond between us.

When Bro Eze learned that I was serving as a corps member at the college, he went out of his way to find me and introduce himself. At that time, I was grappling with accommodation issues, and though we had never met before, he welcomed me into his home with open arms. He understood my struggles, perhaps better than anyone, and offered his help without expecting anything in return.

Despite his modest salary as a teacher, Bro Eze treated me as if I were his own family. He provided me with food, a place to stay, and went above and beyond to ensure my comfort. His generosity was boundless—he would spend his last dime to make sure I was well cared for, never considering his own needs before mine.

Bro Eze's empathy was unmatched. He never wanted me to feel alone or unsupported, especially given the unique challenges we both faced as visually impaired individuals. He understood that while the world might sometimes be harsh, the kindness of one person could make all the difference. In moments of doubt, frustration, or loneliness, he was there to lift my spirits and remind me of the goodness that still existed in the world.

During the one year we spent together, we created a friendship that felt more like family. His house was my home, and his heart was always open to me. I can confidently say that, after God, no one else has shown me the kind of love, care, and selflessness that I experienced with Bro Eze. He was a true embodiment of the belief that love and kindness know no boundaries. His compassion and generosity have left an indelible mark on my life, one that I will carry with me forever.

A Crush, a Trip, and a Painful Ankle

There's one unforgettable experience etched in my memory that never fails to make me smile. One evening, as I sauntered down the street, I overheard a group of ladies chatting animatedly as they walked towards me. As they drew closer, I realized they were discussing none other than—yours truly! They were marveling at how cute and handsome I was, even expressing disbelief that someone like me could be dealing with blindness. I distinctly heard one of them confessing her crush on me. Imagine my heart practically doing somersaults with joy and excitement!

With all this flattering attention, I was flattered but also extremely bashful. My mind was so preoccupied with their praise that I became clumsy. In my distraction, I misjudged my step and awkwardly tripped into a nearby drainage. The pain was instantaneous and intense, as though my ankle had just been subjected to an impromptu snap.

Seeing me in this predicament, the young ladies rushed over with genuine concern. Their reaction was so emotional that two of them actually began to cry. While their sympathy was heartfelt, I was a bit overwhelmed. I'm not one for excessive pity, and their tears made me feel more than a little uncomfortable. All I wanted was to escape and tend to my pain in solitude.

Despite my attempts to gracefully exit the situation, the more I tried to distance myself, the more insistent they became. They were determined to accompany me wherever I was headed. When I told them I was just popping into a nearby shop, they insisted on coming along. With a bit of cash on me, I managed to buy a few small items. But to my dismay, their persistence didn't wane; they offered once again to help me to my hostel.

At this point, my pain was still quite acute, but their company was genuinely enjoyable. I was just trying to avoid drawing too much attention to my discomfort, as I dreaded the thought of excessive sympathy demoralizing me. Realizing they were steadfast in their resolve, I accepted their offer and let them guide me to my hostel.

That day marked the beginning of a wonderful friendship. They were so fond of me that their visits became a daily ritual. They made sure to check in on me every evening, and even though we weren't in the same faculty, they always found a way to assist me to my classes. Their unwavering support was a source of great comfort.

In a delightful twist of fate, one of these remarkable women eventually became my first girlfriend in school. Looking back, I'm filled with gratitude for their kindness and care. That day of mishaps turned into a cherished memory, leading to deep friendships and a joyful chapter in my life.

Sir Michael L: A Stranger's Kindness, A Father's Heart

Finally, I want to mention someone to whom I am deeply indebted—Sir Michael. I have never met him, never heard his voice, yet his presence in my life has been nothing short of extraordinary. In a world where kindness can sometimes feel rare, he stepped in—not just with financial support, but with a heart fully invested in my journey. He has played the role of a father, especially in securing medical appointments and exploring treatment options for my eyesight. His unwavering concern, his guidance, and his willingness to go the extra mile have been a source of strength for me.

Sir, if you ever come across this, please know that my family and I are deeply, deeply grateful. Your kindness has left an imprint on our hearts, and we will never forget it

The Blessing of Relationships

As I reflect on the journey chronicled in this chapter, I am overwhelmed with gratitude. The tapestry of relationships that have woven through my life—family, friends, and the significant connections I have encountered—have been nothing short of a blessing. It's a humbling realization that, though I may have lost my sight, God blessed me with a vision for something far more profound—the beauty of human connection.

Family is indeed a foundation, and my family, unwavering in their love, has been a constant source of strength, hope, and unwavering support. They have lifted me in ways that words can hardly capture, shining a light on the darkest of days and reminding me that I am never alone. My siblings, my parents, and even my extended family—each one of them has contributed to the person I am today. Through their kindness and loyalty, I've learned that no obstacle is too great to overcome when you are wrapped in the warmth of unconditional love.

Equally precious are the friends who have walked with me through the ups and downs of life, each one bringing their own unique light into my world. Benjamin, Christian, and Bro Eze—each one has etched an indelible mark on my heart. Their friendship has been a reminder that true bonds are formed not out of convenience but through shared love, empathy, and mutual support. These remarkable people have not only supported me but have truly shown me what it means to be seen, valued, and cherished.

And then there are the unexpected joys—the laughter, the connections, and the simple moments of genuine kindness that make life so rich. Like the day I tripped in front of those kind-hearted young ladies, a moment that might have been embarrassing but instead blossomed into lasting friendships and a reminder of the delightful twists fate can bring. Who knew that one misstep could lead to such a joyful chapter in my life?

In all of these relationships, I see the fingerprints of God, orchestrating connections that transcend circumstances. They have been the hands that helped me rise, the shoulders I leaned on, and the hearts that have kept me going. My sight may have been taken, but in the grand scheme, I have been blessed with a far clearer view of the importance of love and human connection.

So, as I close this chapter, I do so with a heart full of gratitude. I am grateful for the people who have walked beside me, the ones who continue to stand with me, and the ones I have yet to meet. May we all be reminded that, regardless of the trials we face, the greatest blessing in life is the relationships we cultivate. For in them, we find strength, solace, and the unwavering belief that no journey is ever too long when shared with others.

Chapter 11:
MY LOVE LIFE

Love—one of the most profound and transformative experiences known to humankind. It is the force that binds souls, the language that speaks even in silence, and the warmth that lingers long after words have faded. Romantic relationships have the power to shape us, to awaken the deepest parts of our hearts, and to remind us that we are not meant to journey through life alone.

For many, love is a thrilling adventure—filled with whispered affections, stolen glances, and the unshakable certainty of belonging to someone. It is the comfort of knowing that no matter how turbulent the storm, there is a hand to hold, a heart that beats in rhythm with yours. It is both the greatest vulnerability and the deepest strength, a paradox that makes life richer and more meaningful.

Yet, for me, love was a longing met with resistance. While my heart yearned for companionship, I grew up in a home where romantic relationships were viewed through the strict lens of conservative Christian values. My parents believed that dating—especially in one's youth—was a distraction, an unnecessary indulgence that could lead down a perilous path. It was something they strongly frowned upon, making it a forbidden desire I dared not openly express.

Many of my peers had girlfriends, navigating the world of love with the reckless excitement of youth. I envied them at times, wondering what it felt like to be chosen, to be cherished in that special way. But for me, the thought of entering a relationship was not just daunting—it was dangerous. If my father ever found out, there would be consequences, and I was not ready to face them.

Mary – My First Love

At 17, I found myself navigating the uncharted waters of my first serious relationship, all thanks to a summer trip to my grandmother's house after my junior class exams. Now, unlike my dad, my grandmother was less of a drill sergeant, and that meant more freedom to explore the complexities of... well, love.

Enter Mary, my first girlfriend, a dazzling combination of beauty, grace, and everything I could ever dream of in a woman. She was one of my cousin sisters' friends, and I first met her during one of those perfectly ordinary visits. But that day? That day was different. The moment our eyes locked, something clicked. I felt it—an undeniable connection, like a spark in the air. She smiled at me, and I couldn't help but notice that the smile wasn't just polite; it was something more, like she was holding a secret that was just for me.

Naturally, I couldn't let this opportunity slip away. I casually asked my cousin sisters about her—hoping for some kind of insight. What I got, however, wasn't quite what I expected. They practically told me to forget it, saying she wasn't into relationships at all. They even threw out names of rich, successful men she had turned down—men who, according to them, stood no chance with her. Their advice? "Find someone easier." I mean, who doesn't love a challenge, right?

Rather than dissuading me, Mary's apparent indifference made me even more determined to win her heart. Slowly but surely, I chipped away at her resistance, and much to my surprise, I found the door to her heart wasn't locked after all. The more we talked, the more we shared, and before I knew it, we were deeply in love—a love that felt like it was written in the stars, destined from the very first glance.

But then came the storm. It wasn't long before my vision started to deteriorate, throwing my world into chaos. In my panic and despair, I turned all my focus toward God, desperate for a miracle, hoping for healing. But as my spiritual journey consumed me, my relationship with Mary started to crumble. The balance I once held between love and faith shattered.

Eventually, I lost Mary. The hurt was deep—agonizing, in fact—but what stung more than anything wasn't the breakup itself. No, what cut to the core was discovering, after all the pain, that she didn't move on to someone else. No, she chose my best friend. Behind my back. It felt like a betrayal so raw it could never heal, leaving a scar that would last for years.

Adak: My Kind Friend.

After the heartbreak of losing Mary, I decided to take a break from love. I gave myself five years to heal, to find peace within myself before even thinking about another relationship. But as they say, life has a way of throwing surprises at you when you least expect them.

And that's when Adak came into the picture.

Now, Adak wasn't just some girl I met—she was the kind of person who changed the very atmosphere when she walked into a room. She wasn't just a friend; she was a beacon of light in a time when I needed it the most. When I met her, I was still adjusting to the harsh realities of losing my sight, trying to find my footing in a world that seemed more daunting than ever.

Adak and her family were regular visitors at the school for the blind where I was trying to get used to my new life. They brought food, support, and something much more important— warmth. The kind of warmth that wrapped around you like a blanket on a cold night.

I remember the exact moment I met her. It was only the second day I was there. She came up to me with that gentle curiosity, like she had all the time in the world to know my story. Before I could even begin to explain my journey, she was already listening. It was a simple question, "What happened to you?" But the way she asked, with that deep empathy, made me feel seen in a way I hadn't in a long time.

That moment marked the beginning of a friendship that would soon evolve into something much deeper.

But, of course, every light casts a shadow. Some of the other students, who had grown used to Adak's attention, didn't take too kindly to how she started focusing on me. I wasn't blind to the jealousy brewing among my peers—Adak had always been a friend to everyone. But after we met, she shifted her attention almost entirely to me. She brought me food, checked in on me, and made sure I was okay... but not everyone was as thrilled about it as I was.

I could feel the weight of their eyes on me, and I couldn't just sit back and let my friends feel excluded. So, like any person with half a brain, I sat Adak down and asked her to be mindful of how she spread her kindness. She heard me out, but in true Adak fashion, she didn't change. Her heart was just too big, and she couldn't help but pour it into me.

Despite my concerns, our bond grew stronger. Slowly, but surely, love began to bloom between us—quietly, tenderly, like flowers in spring. Adak became my rock, my confidante, and my constant source of comfort. She made me feel seen and loved in a world that had made me feel invisible.

But while her love was everything I needed, I wasn't quite ready for what she envisioned for us. She spoke of marriage and a future together, painting a picture so beautiful it almost felt real. And though I wanted to believe in it with all my heart, I knew deep down that I wasn't there yet. I loved her, deeply, but I was young, just starting out in the special school, with nothing to my name. My future was a vast, uncertain expanse, and the very idea of marriage felt overwhelming—a commitment I had no means to honor. How could I promise forever when I was still trying to find my footing in the present?

Even so, Adak's place in my life was undeniable. She had helped me rediscover a part of myself that I thought I had lost— my self-worth. Before her, I had convinced myself that love was something I'd never find again, especially not with someone who could see. But she showed me that love isn't defined by physical sight—it's the sight of the soul that matters.

Adak was the one who helped me rebuild my confidence, brick by brick, reminding me that I was worthy of love, of respect, and of a future filled with joy.

She was the light that pierced through the darkness of my uncertainty, a reminder that even in life's toughest seasons, there's always room for love, friendship, and hope. For all of that, and so much more, I will forever be grateful for Adak. She was my gift when I needed it the most.

The Pursuit of True Love

During my final year at university, I found love again with a wonderful lady named Goodness, who truly embodied her name. We were deeply in love and hoped to marry. However, she wanted to get married immediately after graduation, while I was not financially ready. Though I loved her dearly, I couldn't in good conscience enter a marriage without being able to provide for my family. With a heavy heart, I encouraged her to move on and find someone ready for marriage. Once again, my dream of settling down was shattered—not by our lack of love, but by financial limitations.

Then came my Joy

After graduation, I had the pleasure of meeting another incredible woman, Joy, during my National Youth Service. Meeting Joy was like running into a burst of sunshine on a cloudy day. The moment our paths crossed, there was this immediate warmth between us, almost like we had been friends for years. Turns out, we were both from the same state, which, in my book, made our connection feel like fate had sent us a friendship request and I happily hit "accept." Though I once entertained the idea of marriage (don't get too excited, though) I quickly realized that Joy had a boyfriend—life, always playing the plot twist. Still, that didn't make our connection any less special.

Joy became this steady beacon of light in my life, shining brightly even when things felt a little...well, dark. Not only did she have a heart big enough to fit the entire world, but she also had an uncanny ability to swoop in with support right when I needed it most. There were times when I barely had two coins to rub together, and yet, there was Joy, offering to share whatever she had. She gifted me clothes, shoes, and the occasional pep talk, ensuring that I never let my spirits get too low. My wardrobe, once limited to "barely passable," was soon upgraded to something that made me look like I had my life together (spoiler: I didn't).

Her kindness? Well, it was like an all-you-can-eat buffet. From emotional support to spiritual encouragement, and let's not forget the financial help that could have easily passed for "angelic intervention," Joy showed me that true generosity has no price tag. In another universe where things aligned just a little differently, I would have loved the chance to share my life with Joy. But, life being the plot-twister it is, our paths didn't converge that way. And yet, the impact she had on my life? Unforgettable. Joy, along with the other amazing friends I've had the privilege of knowing, brought so much color to my world. It's like my soul went from grayscale to full HD, blooming in ways I never imagined.

God used people like Joy to show me the best version of myself, and for that, I'll always be grateful. So, I hold her in a special place in my heart, forever thankful for the light she brought into my life. She truly made a difference, and for that, she'll always be my favorite plot twist.

My relationship with Rayne

Some love stories are written in ink, steady and sure. Others are scribbled in wildfire, consuming, unpredictable, and leaving only embers in their wake. The latter was my story with Rayne —a tale of longing, chaos, control, and heartbreak that started in 2018, a time when my heart still believed in the sincerity of distant voices, when love seemed like a possibility even across oceans. She was a stranger, an American woman whose words, typed into the emptiness of a Facebook chat, would soon weave themselves into the fabric of my life. A simple "Hello" on Facebook. I had no way of knowing then that this casual greeting would unravel into one of the most dramatic relationships of my life. My careless 'Hi' unraveled a tapestry of passion and pain.

At first, I had no idea whom I was speaking to. The conversation ambled on aimlessly, until she asked, "Do you like fishing?"

I recoiled. Fishing? In Nigeria, it was more than just a profession—it was a test of resilience, battling both the tides and societal perceptions. "A bit uninterested, I nearly walked away. But something—something inexplicable—held me still.

Instead of shutting the door, I asked, "Do you?"

And just like that, she led me into her world— she spoke of serene waters, the tranquility of the waiting, the thrill of the catch. Her words painted images of a world so different from mine, yet, oddly, I was drawn in.

Even then, I didn't know her name. I didn't know her face.

She could have been anyone.

But when I asked, she told me—Rayne, a woman from the United States.

A woman whose voice, when I finally heard it over a Facebook call, erased my doubts in an instant.

That first night, she unraveled before me like a confession whispered in the dark. Her past, riddled with betrayal, neglect, and pain, unfolded between us.

126

She spoke of the fathers of her children—men who had left her to raise them alone.

She spoke of family that called her delusional.

She spoke of a church that had cast her out, a pastor who had deemed her insane when she spoke of the Illuminati and aliens and advised her to seek psychiatric help.

She had lost her faith.

She had lost everything, and in the silence between her sobs, I felt it—her loneliness, raw and unfiltered.

Perhaps it was foolish.

Perhaps it was the part of me that had known suffering, that understood the weight of rejection.

But that night, I made her a promise.

"I will always be here."

And from that moment on, I was.

Every day, my voice reached her across time zones, a thread weaving warmth into the cold places of her life.

And as they say, constant communication breeds affection.

Two weeks was all it took.

She confessed her love, unable to hold back.

And I, despite myself, had already fallen.

For two months, love was sweet.

For two years, love was complicated.

Rayne, generous yet demanding, began testing the strength of my dreams. She spoke of the cost of our calls, of my devotion, questioning how I could afford to call her every day as a student. She wanted to reciprocate, and I appreciated her concern and thoughtfulness. So she sent me money—not much, but enough to make me grateful. Enough to make me feel indebted. I received $100. Over the years, that total grew to $350—not a fortune, but a symbol of her desire to keep me tethered.

But love, when laced with expectation, quickly turns into a chain. Rayne wanted more than my words—she wanted my presence. She begged me to abandon my education and move to the U.S., promising $1,000 upon my arrival. I asked her to be patient—I was still in my 200 level at the university—but Rayne wouldn't hear of it. She insisted that education was useless to me.

But I couldn't just throw away my future. Abandoning my studies would not only disappoint my parents, but it would also leave me without a solid foundation. A degree wasn't just a piece of paper; it was security, something I could rely on no matter what happened. Besides, how could I gamble everything on a life I wasn't even sure of? Moving far away from everything familiar, for someone I had never met in person, felt too risky. A bird in hand is worth more than a thousand in the bush. I needed something certain, something real. Finishing university was just a matter of a few more years, and I was determined to see it through.

But Rayne refused to understand. She became volatile. Love twisted into accusations, devotion curdled into demands. Her affection turned to rage.

She called me selfish. Ungrateful. A user of her kindness.

Her words, once tender, became sharp as knives. Until, at last, it all fell apart. Yelling, insults, curses—the relationship cracked, splintered. Our love story darkened. After two years, we crumbled.

Rayne's Call and the TV Show Opportunity

Three years had passed since I broke up with Rayne—since our relationship crumbled like a house built on sand. I had moved on—or so I thought—until one fateful Wednesday afternoon, my slumber was interrupted by a call. Not just any call, but one from an international number.

My little phone, a humble gift from my dear brother Eze after I lost my smartphone, vibrated aggressively in my palm. Groggy and caught between the dream world and reality,

Curiosity won over my drowsiness. I picked up the call.
"Hello?

A voice I hadn't heard in years sliced through the silence—Rayne's. But instead of the warmth one would expect after such a long absence, she sounded rushed, almost as if she were reading from a script.

"I don't have much time. Listen, I applied for *90 Day Fiancé*, and we've been selected."

I sat up instantly, my heartbeat accelerating. "Wait, what? We?"

She sighed, impatient. "Yes, you and me. It's a reality TV show in America. Big opportunity. Get ready they are going to call you"

I didn't understand any word of it, so, I borrowed a smart phone and called her back, I explained to her that I didn't have a smart phone.

I had never even heard of the show, let alone imagined myself on it. Was she serious? Or was this one of those dreams where the most absurd things seemed plausible?

But days later, my skepticism turned to stunned reality when the production company called me directly. They spoke about auditions, background checks, and a contract. To my surprise, I passed all of it.

I should have been ecstatic. And at first, I was. But excitement was quickly overshadowed by a more pressing issue: I didn't have a smartphone, which meant I couldn't communicate effectively with the producers. Borrowing a phone from a neighbor was awkward at best and risky at worst; given my visual impairment, borrowing it for professional video interviews was another level of discomfort.

Eventually, even Rayne found the situation unbearable. She sent me money to buy a smartphone—a kind gesture, which I appreciated. But knowing Rayne, there was always something behind her generosity. And I wasn't wrong.

A Love That Wasn't Quite Love

Dating Rayne had been a paradox—an enigma wrapped in bittersweet memories. Losing my sight was one of the hardest things I had ever endured, but my relationship with her came in at a close second. It had been a whirlwind of passion, misunderstandings, love, control and pain. And yet, ironically, here she was, pulling me into one of the greatest opportunities of my life. If not for her, I wouldn't have been considered for the show. But that didn't erase the wounds she had left behind.

Our first relationship had been intense, filled with deeply romantic and erotic conversations. But when she resurfaced after three years, it was as if I had forgotten all that led to our break up, we decided to rewrite our story, to create something new from the ashes of what had been. But I had changed. I made her understand that my faith had transformed me. I had taken a vow of celibacy, when she arrived, we would not be sleeping together. There would be no blurred lines, no whispered temptations in the dark. I made this clear to her.

Rayne didn't take it well. It was a reality she found too hard to accept. She raged, cursed, and cried. She threatened to cancel her trip, blocked me, then unblocked me—an emotional whirlwind that I mistook for the tantrum of a woman in love. But I was wrong. It wasn't just affection she craved; it was control.

I realized this when I received a call from one of the producers asking if I knew a man named Emmanuel. My breath caught. I did know him—we had attended the same special school for the blind. And now, I was learning that on the very night she had blocked me, Rayne had called the producer, attempting to replace me with him.

She had reached out to Emmanuel, asking how close he was to Lagos, inquiring whether he could be the one by her side instead. But the producer refused. Emmanuel wasn't under contract, and the show had already been set. Only then did Rayne abandon her plan and return to me, as if nothing had happened.

Her actions forced me to confront an unsettling question: Had she come back for love, or was I merely a stepping stone to her dream of being on television? She had always wanted to be on TV. Was I just a convenient means to an end?

When she realized there was no way to change my mind, Rayne relented—perhaps hoping she could bend me to her will once she arrived. The show later portrayed it as though I had never told her about my celibacy, but the truth was, I had.

The world saw a woman scorned, blindsided by a revelation she hadn't expected. But the truth was, Rayne had always known about my celibacy. And still, she came. And still, she tried to break me.

During the filming of the show, Rayne was menacing, manipulative, and insulting—not just to me, but to my family too. A lot happened behind the scenes, and The Rayne the world saw on television was the best version of her. The producers did a fantastic job of concealing her madness. When I stood my ground about celibacy, she resorted to dark threats—ones that made my blood run cold. She said she would take both our lives if she didn't get what she wanted. And she didn't stop there. She directed her rage at my sister, at the producers—at anyone who stood in the way of her desires.

When persuasion failed, she turned to cruelty. She belittled my faith, mocked my devotion, and spewed venom at my sister. I wanted to love this woman, but I was afraid of her. Her touch, which I had hoped would be the source of my greatest pleasure at the right time, had become a threat. I couldn't trust her. She could be sweet as honey, and then turn as vicious as a viper in the next breath. She twisted the truth to fit her desires, spinning lies so effortlessly that even I started to question reality.

I know people can react terribly when they don't get what they want, especially in romantic relationships, but the extent to which Rayne went was both baffling and disheartening to me. I've dealt with difficult people before, but I never imagined someone could be so vicious and hateful, and yet still profess love with their words.

I was shocked during and after the airing of the show to see the lies and allegations Rayne made against me and my sister—just for what?

When she claimed that my sister's house was a fake house rented for the show—a house my sister and her family had lived in for over six years—I was left marveling at the level of hate a woman could have for another woman, especially when there's no rivalry involved. Rayne hated my sister even before meeting her in person. Before she arrived in Nigeria, she constantly complained about the negative energy she felt toward my sister and my entire family. She made it clear that she did not want to meet them—an idea that sounded absurd to me. Family was everything. She confessed that she had expected conflict with any potential sister-in-law, and when she met my sister, she did everything in her power to insult and humiliate her, despite how much Victoria tried to embrace, welcome, and love her. Rayne even went as far as making racist remarks about me and my sister, only to later claim online that my sister had been racist toward her.

Another distortion was the narrative surrounding the gifts I gave her when she was leaving Nigeria. I don't regret giving them. First, she had brought gifts for me, so courtesy demanded that she leave with something in return. Second, she had told me the money she sent for the phone came from her mother, so I bought a small token of appreciation for her mother. Third, Rayne cherished those gifts so much that she later sent me pictures of her son happily using them. Even though she told the world on camera I was using it to manipulate her. In fact, it had slipped my mind to buy something for her daughter, and they bitterly complained about it—so much so that she ended up giving her daughter one of her own gifts. She even later confessed that one of the gifts I gave her made her feel like a lady for the first time in her life.

For all the turmoil she caused, my love for her only grew stronger, People asked why. How could I have held onto a woman who treated me with such disdain? But love is rarely logical. It's a madness of the heart, blindness more profound than any loss of sight. Something about her made me want to stick with her. But whatever that was—it was madness and stupidity on my part.

My family, however, was not so easily fooled. They saw what I refused to see. And they warned me.

But my attachment to Rayne wasn't just about affection—it was also about compassion. Beneath all her chaos and aggression, I had seen in her a broken soul, a woman desperately in need of love and healing. And I had wanted to be part, if not the source of that healing. I wanted to be that help, I wanted to love her. Unfortunately, she was incapable of receiving or even recognizing it.

A Lesson, Not a Lifelong Partner

I didn't want to dwell too much on Rayne because I had moved on to greater opportunities and relationships. But in writing about my experiences, it would be impossible to leave her out. She was, after all, part of the journey.

Life has a way of using even our greatest pains to carve out our destinies. What should have been a terrible mistake—reuniting with Rayne—ended up being an open door to something greater?

Because of her, I was on the show.

Because of her, I met incredible people from around the world.

Because of her, I walked through fire—and came out refined.

Would I have chosen this path for myself? Never! But God, in His infinite wisdom, took what was meant for evil and turned it into good.

Rayne may have thought she was in control, scripting her way into fame. But in the end, the truth prevailed. The cameras stopped rolling, the producers returned to the U.S., and life continued. The difference? I was no longer the same man I had been before that fateful Wednesday afternoon.

If there is one lesson I have learned, it's that not everyone who re-enters your life deserves a second chance. Some people are meant to be lessons, not lifelong partners.

And Rayne? She was the most unforgettable lesson of them all. While I'm grateful that Rayne, crossed ocean to visit me in Nigeria, the truth is that I regret ever getting involved with her in the first place.

Despite everything, I remain grateful. Though I once loved Rayne and wanted to marry her, I now realize how much danger I was blindly walking into. Watching the show opened my eyes, and I thank God I was spared. The show gave me visibility, but more importantly, it helped me reflect on my strengths and weaknesses. You must know that I'm nothing near perfection, a man full of weaknesses and deficiencies. But With all I have learned, I am now wiser, stronger, and more resilient.

Chapter 12:
BREAKING BARRIERS—MY FIRST JOB

If you had told me years ago that I would one day be employed, earning a salary, and making an impact on the lives of others—not just blind folks, but also impacting the lives of my sighted students—I would have found it hard to believe. Not because I lacked the will or determination, but because society often painted a different picture—one where people like me, the visually impaired, were expected to depend on others rather than stand on our own. Seeing my students excited, happy, and eagerly learning from me is one of the greatest thrills of my life—an experience I will forever cherish and be eternally grateful for.

For the longest time, I wrestled with the uncertainty of my future. While I pursued my education with diligence, a question lingered in my heart: *What would I do with this knowledge? Would I ever have the chance to truly use it?* I had heard too many stories of people with disabilities who, despite their intelligence and qualifications, were shut out of opportunities simply because the world didn't see them as capable. For a time, I feared that would be my reality too.

But today, my heart overflows with joy and gratitude because God has proven His faithfulness once again!

I have gained employment! Those words alone feel surreal. The very thing I once thought impossible has now become my reality. I can hardly describe what it means to know that I am earning a salary—no matter how small—through my own effort and skills. It's more than just financial independence; it's the validation that I am capable, that my education was not in vain, and that I have something valuable to offer the world.

I am especially grateful for the opportunity to work as a teacher in a high school in Oyo State. Every day, I step into the classroom with a heart full of purpose, knowing that I am helping shape young minds. It is a rich and rewarding experience to impact the lives of these wonderful students. Their curiosity, enthusiasm, and resilience inspire me as much as I hope to inspire them. Teaching them is more than just a job—it is a calling, a privilege, and a reminder that God can use us in ways we never imagined.

But even more fulfilling than the paycheck is the opportunity to impact lives, especially the younger generation, through teaching. The idea that I get to impart knowledge, guide minds, and inspire others is something I never imagined would happen for me. And yet, here I am, living that reality.

This journey has been nothing short of miraculous. From the uncertainty of wondering what my future held to the overwhelming joy of walking in God's plan, I have seen firsthand that when He makes a way, no obstacle can stand in the path.

To anyone who has ever doubted their potential, to those who feel limited by circumstances—please believe me when I say this: God is faithful. He is not bound by human expectations or limitations. If He could do this for me, He can and will do it for you.

Today, I celebrate this incredible milestone in my life, and I do so with a heart full of gratitude. To everyone who has supported me, encouraged me, and believed in me—even when I struggled to believe in myself—thank you. Your prayers, kindness, and unwavering faith in my journey have played a part in this victory.

This is just the beginning. The best is yet to come! Glory to God!

Chapter 13:
CHIDI LIGHT EMPOWERMENT FOUNDATION FOR THE BLIND

As I reflect on my journey, I am deeply humbled by the grace of God that has guided me from the depths of despair to the heights of purpose. This journey, marked by resilience, courage, and unwavering faith, has been more than just a personal triumph—it has been a show of the power of hope and the potential within each of us, regardless of the challenges we face.

The blind, the society, and my vision

My deep curiosity about the societal factors hindering the progress and integration of persons with disabilities led me to pursue a degree in Sociology. This academic path was driven by a desire to understand and address the barriers faced by individuals with disabilities, especially those with visual impairments. However, I quickly realized that academic knowledge alone wasn't enough to create the change I envisioned. My experiences revealed a pervasive pity toward those with disabilities, coupled with a glaring lack of understanding and awareness about their abilities and rights. This societal blindness, which often manifests in demeaning questions and negative perspectives, constitutes one of the greatest obstacles we face in Nigeria.

Despite commendable steps by the Nigerian government, such as the establishment of the National Disability Commission and the enactment of the National Disability Rights Law, many individuals with disabilities remain marginalized. Poverty, lack of resources, and societal misunderstanding continue to limit their potential. Driven by this reality and the hope for a better future, I pursued a Master's degree in Social Work to deepen my understanding of how to support individuals with disabilities through practical interventions.

The trials I have endured were not solely for my own growth but to equip me to serve others, especially those who share my experience of visual impairment. God has lifted me up, not for personal gain, but to be a vessel through which His blessings can flow to others. It is this sense of purpose that has driven me to establish the CHIDI LIGHT EMPOWERNMENT FOUNDATION FOR THE BLIND.

The foundation is more than just an organization; it is a movement born out of gratitude for the grace that has sustained me and the support that has empowered me. My visibility, particularly as the first blind person featured on TLC's *Before 90 Days*, is a platform entrusted to me not just for my own story, but to shine a light on the stories of countless others who face similar struggles but lack the opportunities I have been given.

Through the Chidi LIGHT Empowerment Foundation, we aim to address the systemic barriers that continue to marginalize individuals with visual impairments. Our mission is to bridge the gap between their potential and the opportunities available to them by providing essential resources, including assistive technologies like computers with screen readers, smartphones with accessibility features, and Braille devices. We also offer educational programs to ensure these tools are used effectively.

But we cannot do this alone. This foundation, grounded in the lessons of my own journey and bolstered by my academic and practical experiences, is a call to action for all who believe in the dignity and potential of every human being. I invite you to join us in this mission. Whether through donations, partnerships, or simply spreading the word, your support can transform lives. Together, we can create a world where individuals with visual impairments have the same opportunities to succeed, thrive, and contribute to society as anyone else.

Reflecting on my past, I see a story not just of personal victory, but of a collective journey toward a more inclusive and

138

compassionate world. This is our story—a story of hope overcoming despair, inspiration triumphing over adversity, and faith conquering fear. As we move forward, I am filled with gratitude for every challenge, every victory, and every person who has walked this path with me.

Thank you for being part of this journey. With your help, the Chidi LIGHT Empowerment Foundation for the Blind will continue to shine brightly, offering a new narrative for individuals with disabilities—one of empowerment, dignity, and boundless potential.

Chapter 14:
WHY I SET UP THE GOFUNDME

From the moment I lost my sight, I carried a deep longing—a prayer whispered in faith—for the chance to access advanced medical treatment. Unfortunately, this hope seemed out of reach in Nigeria, as local doctors told me there was nothing that could be done. Yet, despite their words, I never stopped believing that there had to be more.

After appearing on the show, something remarkable happened. I was overwhelmed by messages from kind-hearted individuals around the world, many of whom shared groundbreaking advancements in vision restoration. Some sent me links to cutting-edge research, while others connected me with specialists who offered hope where I had been told there was none. Their words reignited something in me—a renewed belief that my journey was far from over.

I remain convinced that I have never received a proper diagnosis or adequate medical intervention. And I truly believe that if I am examined by the right specialists, there is still a chance—perhaps not to regain everything, but even the possibility of partial restoration is worth pursuing. If, in the rare case, nothing can be done, at least I will have peace knowing that every effort was made. It would fulfill not only my own longing but also my father's deepest wish—a wish he held onto until his final breath.

Looking back on my life, the many challenges I've faced, and the victories I've won, I realize that my faith has only grown stronger. God has brought me this far, and I refuse to limit His power. I still believe in miracles. But I also believe that faith without action is incomplete. That is why I've taken this bold step—to walk through the door God has opened for me.

By His grace, after much effort, I've secured an appointment at Moorfields Eye Hospital in the United Kingdom—one of the world's leading and most renowned eye clinics—for an advanced prognosis and possible treatment. This long-awaited medical trip is set to take place before the middle of the year, marking a critical step in my journey toward finding answers and exploring the best available options for my sight. This is an opportunity I cannot afford to miss, and I trust God will complete the work He has started.

However, this journey is about more than just my sight. It's about a greater vision—one that extends beyond myself. It's about empowering others who, like me, have faced the darkness but refuse to be defined by it. That's why I founded the Chidi Light Empowerment Foundation for the Blind—to offer education, assistive technology, and vocational training to visually impaired individuals.

If, for any reason, medical treatment is not viable, I want every donor to know that the funds raised will not go to waste. They will be directed into the foundation, supporting others who need help. Together, we can create a brighter future for those who face the same challenges I've faced.

To everyone who has already contributed to my GoFundMe, I cannot express my gratitude enough. Your generosity and belief in this journey mean more than I can say. Whether your donation is toward my medical treatment or the foundation's mission, please know that you are making a lasting impact.

I pray that God blesses you abundantly, replenishes your resources, and grants you favor in all that you do. This is more than a medical journey—it's an demonstration of faith, hope, and the power of community. With your continued support, I know the best is yet to come.

Thank you, from the depths of my heart.

Conclusion:
THE ROAD AHEAD: A PROMISE TO THE FUTURE

As I close this chapter of my story, I do so with a heart full of hope, love, and unwavering faith. The past I have shared is what I know, what I have lived, and what I have come to understand about myself so far. But I know my story is far from over. There is more to unfold—more lessons, more victories, more impact, more love, and more life waiting ahead.

To my future wife, wherever you are, know that I have prayed for you, dreamed of you, and prepared my heart to love you as Christ loves the Church. I do not promise perfection, but I vow to cherish you, honor you, and create a home where love is unwavering and joy overflows. By God's grace, I will make our marriage a taste of heaven on earth—a bond rooted in faith, nourished by kindness, and strengthened through every season we face together. You will never walk alone, for I will stand beside you as your greatest admirer, your safest place, and your unshakable partner in this journey of life.

To my future children, you are already loved beyond words. I long to hold you, to guide you, and to teach you the lessons life has taught me. I promise to be a father who is present—not just in body, but in heart, mind, and spirit. Our home will be one of love, wisdom, laughter, and purpose—a haven where you will be nurtured, encouraged, and equipped to fulfill your God-given destinies. I will pour into you the riches of my experiences, teaching you to walk in faith, resilience, and grace. You will never lack love, and no matter where life takes you, you will always have a father who believes in you.

To my mother, the woman whose prayers, sacrifices, and unwavering faith have carried me through life's hardest moments—I am forever grateful. You are the reflection of God's love on earth, a mother whose strength has been my foundation. You have endured so much, yet you have never stopped giving, never stopped believing, and never stopped loving. I vow to honor you, to make you proud, and to show you that every tear, every prayer, and every sacrifice was not in vain. May God bless you abundantly for all you have done.

To my siblings, my first friends and lifelong confidants, you have been my strength in ways I cannot fully express. Through every season, you have stood by me, cheered for me, and loved me without condition. I am blessed beyond words to have you, and I promise to be the best brother I can be—to celebrate your victories, stand with you in struggles, and ensure that no matter where life takes us, our bond remains unbreakable.

To my friends, my brothers, and my comrades, thank you for walking with me through the highs and lows of my journey. You have been my strength, my joy, and my family beyond blood. I promise to be a better friend, to stand by you as you have stood by me, to celebrate your wins as my own, and to be a refuge in your storms. Life is too fleeting to take friendships for granted, and I vow to cherish every bond that has shaped me.

Beyond my personal dreams, I have a greater purpose—to serve, to uplift, and to leave the world better than I found it. My heart beats for those who, like me, have faced obstacles that seemed impossible to overcome. I will dedicate my life to advocating for the visually impaired, the disabled, and the forgotten, ensuring they have access to the resources, education, and opportunities they deserve. Disability will never define me, nor will I allow it to define others. We are more than our limitations—we are purpose-filled, capable, and destined for greatness.

To my fellow believers, hold fast to your faith. No matter how dark the night, how fierce the storm, or how uncertain the road ahead, never lose sight of the One who holds the future. This world is fleeting, and we are only passing through, but what awaits us is far greater than anything we could ever imagine. It is my deepest prayer and greatest hope that when the trumpet sounds, when the skies break open and our Savior returns in glory, we will all stand together in His presence—redeemed, victorious, and home at last.

I yearn for a life well-lived, a life where I do not merely exist but truly live—to love, to build, to grow, to experience real joy, to have family, to find independence, and to leave a mark that outlives me. No matter how small or grand my impact may seem, I will do my part to make the world a better place.

This is not just the conclusion of my book—it is the beginning of the rest of my story. I step forward with faith, knowing that my future is filled with blessings, impact, and greatness yet to be revealed.

And to God, my ever-faithful Father, I surrender it all. Every dream, every hope, every step—I place them in Your hands. Let my life be a testament to Your grace.

With all my heart,

Chidi Emmanuel Ikpeamaeze

APPRECIATION

I begin by giving my deepest thanks to God, whose unending grace and guidance have made every step of my journey possible. His love and faithfulness have been my strength through it all.

To my family, your unwavering support and love have carried me through every challenge. I am deeply grateful for your presence and the solid foundation you've provided.

A special thank you to my dear sister and editor, Victoria. You are not just intelligent—you are gifted. Your guidance, patience, love, and kindness have been immeasurable throughout my journey. You've not only lent your incredible skills but also your heart, always offering a listening ear and thoughtful contributions that shaped this book. Your care and dedication have truly brought this project to life, and I am forever grateful to have you by my side.

A heartfelt thank you to my incredible network of friends for their constant support. Your encouragement, prayers, and belief in me have been a source of strength, and I am grateful for every word of advice, every act of kindness, and every moment of friendship.

To my dear readers, thank you for taking this journey with me. Your time, your attention, and your willingness to walk through my story mean more than I can express. I pray that within these pages, you found inspiration, encouragement, and a reminder that faith, resilience, and love can carry us through life's greatest challenges.

Lastly, to everyone who has been a part of this journey—whether through prayers, encouragement, or support—thank you. This book is as much yours as it is mine. God bless you.

ABOUT THE AUTHOR

Chidi Emmanuel Ikpeamaeze is a writer, advocate, and educator whose life story is a reflection of grace, resilience and purpose. Born on April 4, 1990, in Obingwa LGA, Aba, Abia State, he lost his sight at 17 but refused to let adversity define his future. He pursued higher education, earning a degree in Sociology and a master's degree in Social Work from the University of Lagos.

A passionate storyteller, Chidi uses his writing to illuminate themes of perseverance, faith, and triumph over life's challenges. His works offer deep insights into the human spirit, drawing from his personal experiences and his commitment to advocacy. As the founder of Chidi Light Foundation for the Blind, he actively promotes inclusivity for visually impaired individuals, equipping them with assistive technology and opportunities for growth.

Beyond writing and advocacy, Chidi is a dedicated educator, currently serving as a senior high school teacher. Through his books, he hopes to inspire, educate, and empower others to rise above their circumstances and embrace their full potential.

Made in United States
Orlando, FL
03 April 2025